VOCABULARY

A KEY TO BETTER
COLLEGE READING

Prentice-Hall International, Inc., *London*
Prentice-Hall of Australia, Pty. Ltd., *Sydney*
Prentice-Hall of Canada, Ltd., *Toronto*
Prentice-Hall of India Private Limited, *New Delhi*
Prentice-Hall of Japan, Inc., *Tokyo*

VOCABULARY
A KEY TO BETTER
COLLEGE READING

Thomas E. Nealon
Frederick J. Sieger

*Reading Department
Nassau Community College*

Prentice-Hall, Inc.
Englewood Cliffs, New Jersey

TO OUR WIVES, CAROL AND LILLIAN

13-942953-0

Library of Congress Catalog Card Number: 70-115779

Printed in the United States of America

Current Printing (last digit):

10 9 8 7 6 5 4 3 2 1

CONTENTS

UNIT II

USE OF DICTIONARY

UNIT III

LATIN AFFIXES—PREFIXES AND SUFFIXES

UNIT IV

THE DEVELOPMENT OF THE ENGLISH LANGUAGE—LATIN ROOTS

UNIT V

THE GREEK CONTRIBUTION—GREEK PREFIXES AND ROOTS

PREFACE

To The Student

The miracle of language is that people are able to express ideas, emotions, thoughts, and observations through the medium of printed and spoken symbols. Often, gestures, tone of voice, and even facial expressions may influence and give special emphasis to a lecture. Words, with meaning, and in their proper order, are the vehicles that chronicle history, move multitudes, and establish intelligent lines of communication.

For the student, working with this miracle of language is often a frustrating experience if he does not have at his command the precise word that will make the sentence "go," the specific word that clarifies his own thoughts. A weakness in vocabulary often thwarts the completion of a really excellent term paper. Lacking a "feel" for words, a student cannot come to grips with basic concepts expressed in science, history, philosophy texts, etc. It is for this reason that *Vocabulary: A Key to Better College Reading* attempts to generate some enthusiasm for vocabulary study.

Dealing with etymologies, Latin and Greek affixes and roots that have affected the English language, students may come to appreciate word structure and, above all, arrive at an understanding that words have shades and degrees of meaning. Constant reinforcement through practice exercises is the practical means used to achieve this goal. Many of the words will be found in college texts, and the general discussions concerning language development should be of interest. An astronaut in space requires special equipment and sophisticated tools to perform required tasks. Ultimate success depends on such material and its effective use. Likewise a rich, deep vocabulary is the vehicle to greater understanding of the sociology discussion, the English essay, and the scientific article. Getting to the heart of the matter requires first, a familiarity and an awareness of denotations and connotations of words and second, a sense of confidence in dealing with abstract terms—both of which may come from an intensive study of vocabulary.

Format

Each lesson is followed by at least two exercises. The first, "Exercise A", can be completed in class, usually in about ten minutes. Other than referring to the lesson, and sometimes a dictionary, no special materials are needed. "Exercise B" is intended for homework assignment; it frequently requires the use of a collegiate dictionary. When a lesson is of special importance or interest, a "Supplementary Exercise" is included.

Five addenda of Latin and Greek prefixes and roots follow Lesson 30. For easy reference they are arranged in alphabetical order.

Acknowledgments

The authors would like to acknowledge those students who, although they will never read this book in its published form, have contributed greatly to its existence. For almost five years they have let us know what they considered to be unfair questions, tricky sentences or just "dull stuff." We hope that future students will also take us to task but find much merit in our work.

We would like to take this opportunity to thank our reviewers and critics whose criticisms were fair and constructive. They have made this not only a book but also a much better book. They are Professor Joan G. Roloff of William Rainey Harper Junior College, Palatine, Illinois; Professor Rose Marks, American River College, Sacramento, California; Professor Henry L. Copps, Jr., Polk Junior College, Winter Haven, Florida; and Professor Teresa Glazier, College of San Mateo, San Mateo, California. In addition we would like to thank Dr. Harvey Alpert, Hofstra University, Hempstead, New York, for his encouragement after the initial reading. Lastly, our indebtedness is especially due to our colleague, Mr. John Keaney, Reading Supervisor of the East Meadow School District, New York, who contributed to the final reading of the manuscript.

T.E.N.
F.J.S.

INTRODUCTION

In a very real sense America, despite its varied cultures, is a land that has no language barrier. From coast to coast communication is possible through conversation, radio, movies, television, magazines, and newspapers. Even the foreign born put special emphasis on learning the language. Consequently, a high degree of literacy should be one of the hallmarks of our society. Yet, the ordinary person and, unfortunately, many of our average college students never really move beyond the simple to the more complex and more refined usages of our English vocabulary. Joseph Conrad once remarked: "Give me the right word and the right accent and I will move the world." This is even more true today for the effective knowledge of words is the key to an understanding of social, scientific, political, and international problems.

The practical results and the intangible benefits you can accrue from a systematic study of vocabulary are well worth your effort.

1) Effective word study can influence your everyday speech and writing.

2) The exact word to express your precise thought will enable you to be better understood in speaking and writing.

3) Words, for the most part, will no longer be obstacles to your reading progress; your reading rate and comprehension will improve.

4) Since words stand for ideas, as well as things, a fundamental grasp of shades of meaning is necessary for any form of communication—reading, writing, speaking, and listening.

5) Be on good terms with words in order to improve your school work, to write better themes, to be more confident in examinations; to be an educated person.

6) Your choice of words often reflects your personality traits.

7) Inadequate vocabulary is a blind spot in your educational arsenal that can and should be eliminated.

To achieve some or all of the above goals you should systematically organize your study of vocabulary. The approach used in the following example represents effective techniques for analyzing a difficult but meaningful passage.

Arnold Bennett in his essay, "On Literary Taste," expressed a common sense approach to the study of literature. "I wish particularly that my readers should not be *intimidated* by the apparent vastness and *complexity* of this enterprise of forming the literary taste. It is not so vast nor so complex as it looks. There is no need whatever for the inexperienced enthusiast to confuse or frighten himself with thoughts of 'literature in all its branches.' The idea of the unity of literature should be well planted and *fostered* in the head. All literature is the expression of feeling, of passion, of emotion, caused by the sensation of the interestingness of life."

There are four aids to understanding all of the words, and therefore all of the meaning, of this paragraph.

CONTEXT

Context is the setting in which the word or phrase is used: Meaning is based on specific words or ideas in the same sentence, the paragraph, or other parts of the selection.

> *intimidated*—Words like "vastness," "confuse," and "frighten" indicate that the word "intimidated" means something to be feared.
> Actually, Bennett, in stating "should not be" and "no need," wants the reader to take a positive attitude toward the study of literature.
> *fostered*—Connected with well-planted, indicating growth.

STRUCTURE

Structure is the *form* and *development* of a word: This includes the base or root of the word, prefixes and suffixes (affixes), and inflectional ending.

a) *intimidated*
   in—prefix meaning in, within, into, toward,
   timidus (L)—fearful, faint-hearted
   ed—inflectional verb ending
b) *complexity*
   com—prefix meaning with
   plexus (L)—to twist around, entwine
   ity—suffix meaning state of or condition

DICTIONARY

A third aid is the dictionary. In addition to a basic meaning the dictionary often supplies the origin and the history of a word, as in these sample entries.

a) *odyssey* (n)

(the "Odyssey," epic poem attributed to Homer recounting the long wanderings of Odysseus): a long wandering usually marked by many changes of fortune.

See also Odysseus (n)(GK): a king of Ithaca and Greek leader in the Trojan war whose ten-year wanderings after the war are recounted in Homer's *Odyssey*.

b) *virtue* (n)

[This word shows the type of historical development that occurs in many English words.]

Virtus (L) from "vir" a grown man

(1) courage, strength in war. (Since Rome was constantly struggling for survival the concept of warlike activity was commonly found in the language.)

(2) manliness—a generalization to include all good qualities.

(3) moral excellence, as "the virtue of failure."

ASK SOMEONE . . .

Finally, ask a friend or your instructor. Very often we can save time by checking with another student who has a keen interest in a particular subject. A discussion of a word or phrase meaning may add depth and interest to our study.

In summary, if your eyes and mind are word-conscious, new avenues of intellectual attainment will be traveled and your studies will be enhanced by the keener insight which a larger vocabulary will provide.

LESSON 1

SO WHAT MAKES THEM IMMORTAL?

*WORDS DERIVED FROM
PROPER NOUNS*

Man is born today, lives for a moment, and is forgotten tomorrow! Although everyone strives for immortality, history demonstrates that few men ever achieve or attain this elusive goal. Among these few are certain people who not only live in posterity but who also have become part of our language. In all phases of our education we are constantly being brought into contact with references, allusions and even derivations of famous or infamous people and places. From the Bible we have derived such word-names as Job, the symbol of patience; Solomon, personified wisdom; Jezebel, a notoriously wicked woman; Judas, the traitor. Elizabeth I and Victoria so dominated their eras that we refer to the art, literature, history, customs, etc. of their times as Elizabethian and Victorian. Some ancient Greek philosophers live on not only in their discipline but also in such phrases as Platonic love, Socratic dialogue and the Pythagorean theorem. History has produced such words and phrases as kaiser from Julius Caesar, a Pyrrhic victory and the Von Hindenberg line. And, of course, scientists and inventors seem to reap the success of their discoveries by immortalizing themselves in their new terminologies and so we have pasteurization, the Salk vaccine, diesel, watts, and the Van Allen belt, to name but a few.

Many place names have also contributed to the enrichment of our language. History has provided such words and phrases as marathon, cross the Rubicon, spartan, and meet one's Waterloo. In literature we have taken limerick from Ireland, sardonic from the island of Sardinia, and serendipity from Walpole's tale, *The Three Princes of Serendip.* And we are all familiar with the products attributed to the village of Shillelagh, Ireland; the town of Spa, Belgium; the city of

Fez, Morocco; the island of Java, Indonesia; and the state of Kashmir, India.

Many students tend to skip over these proper noun derivations for, they reason, the meaning of one word is certainly not that important. But in so doing they are denying themselves one of the most fascinating aspects of the science of etymology. Who was this person? What gave him or her the right to the immortality that our language has bestowed? How has this word developed this particular meaning?

One of the greatest compliments that can be paid to a tour-guide is that you refer to him as a *cicerone*. Most dictionaries will trace the etymology of this word to Cicero and provide you with its modern meaning. But was Cicero a conductor of tours into Rome's famous catacombs? Plutarch in his chapter on "Cicero" gives us some insight into the basis for the coining of *cicerone*.

> He, Cicero, stated his objections against the law in the senate and effectually silenced the proposers. They took another opportunity, however, and coming prepared, insisted that the consul should appear before the assembly of the people... He addressed the commons with such success that they threw out the bill, and his victorious eloquence had such an effect upon the tribunes that they abandoned other projects which they had been meditating.
>
> Cicero was, indeed, the man who most effectually showed the Romans what charm eloquence can add to truth....[1]

A cicerone is, indeed, a very special kind of tour-guide.

[1] Edward C. Lindeman, ed., *Life Stories of Men Who Shaped History from Plutarch's Lives* (New York: Mentor Books, 1962), pp. 135-36.

EXERCISE A

SOME "HALLOWED" PLACES

Direction: Here is a list of some derivations from famous or infamous places in history and literature. They are identified for you. After you have studied the words, complete sentences 1 to 10, then *return* to the list and write your own definition for the words.

Example:

bedlam   From the Hospital of St. Mary's of Bethlehem for the   *place in*
           insane in London   *an uproar*

During the registration period the college gymnasium, filled with students and professors, not knowing what they were doing and loudly voicing their opinions, was in _____*bedlam*_____.

Athenaeum	From the academy in Rome founded by Hadrian and named for the Greek goddess of wisdom, Athena	a._____
Bunkum	From Buncombe County, N.C., whose congressman made many empty, unimportant speeches on behalf of his people	b._____
Laconic	From Laconian, another name for the Spartans who were renowned for their brevity of speech	c._____
Lilliputian	From the inhabitants, six inches tall, of the Kingdom of Lilliput in *Gulliver's Travels*	d._____
Meandering	From the River Menderes in Asia Minor noted for its winding course	e._____
Mecca	From Mecca, Saudi Arabia, birthplace of Mohammed, the holy city of Islam to which pilgrimages are made	f._____
Pandemonium	In Milton's *Paradise Lost*, the home of the demons, a place of utter confusion	g._____
Stygian	From the mythological River Styx, the principal river of the underworld (the land of the dead)	h._____

3

| Sybarite | From the inhabitants of the Greek city of Sybaris, Italy, notorious for their lavish way of living | i._____ |
| Utopian | From the title of Sir Thomas More's book about an imaginary and highly idealistic community | j._____ |

1. The midget resented being referred to as a _____.

2. The riots caused complete _____ in that part of the city which was already known for its poverty, prostitution and crime.

3. They spent their last afternoon together _____ hand in hand along the river bank.

4. During the spring recess, Fort Lauderdale becomes a _____ for many college students.

5. The young senator proposed a highly desirable but _____ solution for the island government.

6. Lincoln's Gettysburg Address was originally thought to be nothing more than a _____ and uninspiring speech.

7. The new alcove in the library was designated as the special sciences'

_____.

8. The politician's speeches were pure_____, having no practical application for his people.

9. Overnight, with fame and fortune, the starlet's life changed from one of utter poverty to that of a _____.

10. In the bleak, _____ days of the war Churchill rallied his nation to hopefulness and greatness.

4

EXERCISE B

PEOPLE REAL AND FICTITIOUS

Directions: With the aid of your dictionary (a) give the origin and (b) a suitable meaning for each of the words in italics.

Example:

boycott the company   (a) from Captain Charles Boycott, a land agent in County Mayo, Ireland, ostracized by the people for refusing to lower rents.

                                  (b) organized refusal to have dealings with the company.

Different dictionaries provide various background information which is acceptable for the completion of this exercise.

1. . . . *chauvinistic* thoughts about U.S. involvement in Southeast Asia.

   (a)

   (b)

2. . . . the self-styled *Don Juan* of South Hall.

   (a)

   (b)

3. . . . concerned with *Freudian* theories.

   (a)

   (b)

4. . . . accused of attempting to *gerrymander* the state's reapportionment.

   (a)

   (b)

5

5. ... having taken the *Hippocratic* oath.
   (a)

   (b)

6. ... labeled a *jezebel*, completely shameless.
   (a)

   (b)

7. ... a deceitful *Machiavellian* industrialist concerned only with self-advance-ment.
   (a)

   (b)

8. In the classroom Icabod acted the role of the *martinet*, never sparing the rod.
   (a)

   (b)

9. In his *maudlin* condition he appealed to his friend.
   (a)

   (b)

10. ... a congressional *maverick* having no party loyalties.
    (a)

    (b)

11. ... characterized by *Pickwickian* and gullible frame of mind.
    (a)

    (b)

12. ... shot as a *quisling* to his country.

   (a)

   (b)

13. Her *quixotic* solutions were never really considered.

   (a)

   (b)

14. ... his *sadistic* treatment of cats.

   (a)

   (b)

15. The *tawdry* necklace received more praise than was its due.

   (a)

   (b)

SUPPLEMENTARY EXERCISE

Direction: The study of word origins is an intriguing assignment. With the aid of your dictionary (a) give the origin for each italicized word, and then (b) write a meaning for each italicized word.

1. *Bowdlerizing* the text for propriety's sake . . .

   (a)

   (b)

2. . . . a real *dunce*, as stupid as could be.

   (a)

   (b)

3. . . . to lead a sensuous, *epicurean* existence.

   (a)

   (b)

4. . . . A *Falstaffian* comic, more laughed at than with.

   (a)

   (b)

5. Play the game according to *Hoyle*!

   (a)

   (b)

6. . . . a political *philippic*, attacking his opponent's personal life as well as his views . . .

   (a)

   (b)

7. The war in Vietnam may well prove to be only a *Pyrrhic* Victory.

   (a)

   (b)

8. *Serendipity* played a part in many scientific discoveries.

   (a)

   (b)

9. The aristocrat was said to have obtained his bishopric through *simony*.

   (a)

   (b)

10. "Our queer dean" is a *spoonerism* for "our dear queen."

    (a)

    (b)

LESSON 2

"SOMETIMES
HOMER NODS"

*THE ROLE OF GREEK
AND ROMAN MYTHOLOGY
IN LITERATURE*

Everyone appreciates a good story. The tales of mythology are no exception. To appreciate and understand more fully the role of Greek and Roman mythology in literature, we should not be overly concerned with the interpretations given by some scholars. Individual myths may be of some academic interest to various branches of learning, but to the Greeks and to the Romans they were primarily entertaining stories.

Anthropologists and sociologists, through the myths, may find some insights into the lives, cultures and environment of the ancient Greeks and Romans. Some semanticists regard mythology as curious intellectual puzzles in which signs and symbols are to be pieced together. Some psychoanalysts regard them as a collection of sex symbols or weird hallucinations. These interpretations would seem to detract from the imaginative strength of the literature. The world of mythology was not a place of terrors and horrors, but rather one of enjoyment, where a person could laugh at the misfortunes of the gods and thereby forget his own.

Over a hundred years ago Bulfinch, in the introduction to his *Mythology*, attempted to answer those who would see only the "practical" aspects in works of art.

If no other knowledge deserves to be called useful but that which helps to enlarge our possessions or to raise our station in society, then mythology has no claim to that appellation. But if that which tends to make us happier and better can be called useful then we claim that epithet for our subject. For mythology is the handmaid of literature; and literature is one of the best allies of virtue and promoters of happiness.[1]

[1]Fuller, Edmund, ed., *Bulfinch's Mythology* (New York : Dell Publishing Co., 1964), p. 11.

10

This imaginative literature has formed a vast storehouse for some of the best writers of the past twenty-seven centuries. We have found them referred to by our clergy, our dramatists, our politicians, our humanitarians, and especially our poets. But we must not allow these allusions to the myths to change their basic characteristics. The writer as an artist should not draw upon mythology because he lacks originality but rather because he can build upon this great artistic heritage. The name Helen of Troy call forth glamor and romance, love and beauty, and the shortness yet fullness of life.

Many scholars, David Bush, Edith Hamilton and Andrew Lang, for example, see in mythology the beginnings of science. Many of the myths, they say, attempt to explain the feats of nature. Thunder was Zeus hurling his thunderbolts; winter occurs when Prosperpine is in the underworld; the fates of Hyacinthus and Narcissus reveal the origin of these two flowers; etc. But were these stories scientifically true? Should we believe that the great minds of Homer, Sophocles, Virgil and the others meant literally what they wrote? Would we do the same to the brothers Grimm? Ovid (43 B.C.-17 A.D.) himself wrote:

> I spoke of ancient poets' monstrous lies,
> Ne'er seen or now or then by human eyes.

In the Old Testament we read that God created man according to His own image and likeness; however, this was not the idea that the Greeks had. St. Paul, himself a Greek, states that the invisible must be understood by the visible; and so it was that the Greeks made their gods according to their own fancies. Humanized gods and goddesses made for familiarity. Zeus, the highest of the deities, ruled the heavens and the earth with his standards of right and wrong. He severely punished liars and oathbreakers; he was greatly angered by any mistreatment of the dead; yet he himself was constantly trying to hide his various love affairs from his wife and, again and again, he was berated by her. But the Greeks only delighted and enjoyed him the more for his misfortunes. The tales of mythology are pure entertainment, the sort that people of all ages have enjoyed listening to around a fire on a cold wintry evening. They are literature.

"Sometimes Homer nods" is an expression taken from the Latin poet Horace, who felt that in long works like *The Iliad* the author could be expected to have a few lapses—a few drowsy lines. In modern usage it means that we should allow for some mistakes even in the best of us.

EXERCISE A

THE GODS

Here is a list (Column A) of some of the more important Greek and Roman gods and goddesses. A brief explanation of their roles and significance is provided in Column B. After you have studied Columns A and B, complete the sentences. Then return to Column C, writing an appropriate meaning for the word in parentheses.

Column A	Column B	Column C
Example:		
Jove, Jupiter (jovial)	Supreme god of the Romans; his planet was said to have a cheerful influence on mankind	*joyous, happy*
1. Aurora (aurora's tears)	Greek and Roman goddess of dawn	a. _____
2. Bacchus (Bacchanalian)	Roman god of wine	b. _____
3. Eros (erotic)	Greek god of love	c. _____
4. Mars (martial)	Roman god of war	d. _____
5. Mercury (mercurial)	Roman god; swift messenger of the gods.	e. _____
6. Morpheus (morphine)	Roman god of sleep	f. _____
7. Nemesis (nemesis)	Greek goddess of retribution	g. _____
8. Ocrus (ogre)	Roman god of death	h. _____
9. Zephyros (zephyr)	Greek and Roman God of the west wind	i. _____

1. _____ themes in modern movies have led to charges of obscenity and demands for censorship.
2. Boris Karloff, portraying Frankenstein's monster, was probably Hollywood's greatest _____.
3. The marriage feast was a gay and _jovial_ occasion for all.
4. Ruby went to his death asserting that he was Lee Harvey Oswald's _____ and the avenger of Kennedy's assassin.

12

5. Referring to the early morning dew as _____ is a poetic cliché.

6. _____ law was declared and the National Guard moved into the city.

7. The festival in honor of the Greek god Dionysus often turned into a drunken revelry and a _____ orgy.

8. She was constantly administered a large dosage of _____ to deaden the increasing effects of the malignancy.

9. His _____ tendencies made him a poor choice for advancement since he seemed to change with the wind.

10. The soft, gentle _____ made the day ideal for sailing.

EXERCISE B

HEROES AND VILLAINS

Directions: With the aid of the dictionary (a) give the origin and (b) a meaning for each of the italicized words or phrases.

Example:

... a hector, who talks big but doesn't stay to fight.

(a) Hector, son of Priam, bravest of the Trojans
(b) bully

1. Seek his *Achilles' heel* and strike the death blow.

   (a)

   (b)

2. Madame Tabarius, the renowned French journalist *Cassandra*, during Hitler's rise to power in Germany . . .

   (a)

   (b)

3. He avoided receiving a harsh punishment by *giving a sop to Cerberus.*

   (a)

   (b)

4. His *chimerical* writing was grotesque as well as utterly fantastic.

   (a)

   (b)

5. . . . an *elysian* retreat, a second Eden.

   (a)

   (b)

6. . . . to cut the *Gordian knot* . . .

   (a)

   (b)

7. . . . the *Halcyon Days* of yore . . .

   (a)

   (b)

8. . . . burdened with a truly *herculean task*.

   (a)

   (b)

9. . . . to serve as a *mentor* for the poorer students.

   (a)

   (b)

10. Some say that North Vietnam's Ho Chi Minh was a *nestor*.

    (a)

    (b)

11. The story of the *Kon-Tiki* is a modern day *odyssey*.

    (a)

    (b)

12. . . . obsessed with an *oedipus complex*.

    (a)

    (b)

13. The congressman was noted for his *procrustean* tactics.

    (a)

    (b)

14. His *promethean* sacrifices for his fellow men were considered heroic.

    (a)

    (b)

15. ... more than a teaser, a *tantalizer*.

    (a)

    (b)

SUPPLEMENTARY EXERCISE

The names of some of our more interesting foods and beverages have been derived from the places where they attained their first widespread acceptance or where they were actually developed. Locate and list the place where these foods and beverages originated.

Example:
mayonnaise from Port Mahon, Minorea

1. bologna   _____

2. cantaloupe   _____

3. champagne   _____

4. cheddar cheese   _____

5. currants   _____

6. frankfurter   _____

7. gin   _____

8. seltzer water   _____

9. tangerine   _____

10. Waldorf salad   _____

LESSON 3

THE WORLD
OF WORDS

*FOREIGN WORDS BORROWED
INTO ENGLISH*

The history of a language usually reflects the history of a people. With Caesar's conquest in 54 B.C. came the first of the outside influences. In the Anglo-Saxon victory a new language took hold of a large part of Britain. The Viking attackers and the settlers of the ninth century added words from Scandinavia. The Norman Conquest made French the language of the court and, although the Hundred Years' War changed this, a lasting influence has occurred. Wars with the Dutch and the Spanish brought Englishmen in contact with these nationalities and some of their words were adopted. The English involvement with the continental powers enabled French, German, and, to a lesser degree, Russian and Italian words to be borrowed. Many of our most interesting words were brought into the language as a direct result of England's role as an Empire: from the Black Hole of Calcutta to the Rock of Gibraltar, from the sands of the Sahara to the snows of the Himalayas, from the land "down under" to the polar reaches of Canada, from Africa's Gold and Ivory Coasts to the coral isles of the South Pacific and the Caribbean, from the Crown Colony of Hong Kong to the penal colony of Guiana new words were taken into the English language. For three centuries England ruled the Oceans, the Seven Seas, and much that bordered on them. She left an indelible mark—intellectually, culturally, socially—upon the nations which have emerged and are continuing to emerge from her once vast empire. The world has much to be thankful to Britain for, not the least of which is a unique treasury of words without parallel in any other language.

During the course of several generations many borrowed words have been completely Anglicized so that we do not recognize nor do we need to know their etymologies, development of words since their earliest recorded usage. For example, "curfew" is derived from the French words "couvrir" and "feu" meaning to "cover the fire." Because of the great fear of a town's complete destruction by fire—many of the houses were made of wood and had thatched roofs—the town crier would walk through the streets at night directing all fires to be banked.

Words which are only partially Anglicized frequently cause difficulty when adding inflectional endings. The plurals of "alumnus," "stimulus," and "addendum" follow the Latin rules and are "alumni," "stimuli" and "addenda," But the plurals of "curriculum" and "nucleus" may be either "curriculums" or "curricula"; "nucleuses" or "nuclei," And you have TV antennas but sensation organs of insects are antennae. When you are in doubt about a word's inflectional ending, check your dictionary.

EXERCISE A

WHAT'S APROPOS?

Following is a list of some foreign words which have been borrowed directly into the English language. The meanings given are based on the word's etymology; however, in many instances today's commonly accepted meaning is quite different.

For example, *sabotage* is derived from the French *sabot*, "peasant shoe" from which the expression "deliberately working badly," *saboter*, developed. Today, especially in its military connotation, it means to destroy or wreck. "The commandos sabotaged the bridge to prevent the enemy's escape."

Word	Source	Meaning
1. apartheid	Afr.	separateness
2. blitzkrieg	Ger.	lightning and war
3. boudoir	F	to pout; a sulking place
4. cherubs	Heb.	winged heavenly beings
5. dilettante	It.	a person who delights in something
6. furlough	Du.	for leave
7. guerrilla	Sp.	little strife
8. hinterland	Ger.	back country
9. junta	Sp.	joined
10. fiasco	It.	bottle
11. kosher	Heb.	proper, fit
12. pagoda	Pg.	temple

Directions: By using the appropriate "borrowed" word, complete the following sentences as determined by context.

1. In many South American republics the military _____ still control the governments.

2. As choir boys they appeared as _____ but on the ball field they were regular boys.

3. Castro and his men gained control of most of Cuba through _____ tactics.

4. The Union of South Africa has been barred from certain international affairs because of its policy of _____.

5. It is not considered _____ to plagiarize.

20

6. In some areas what was considered the _____, as little as twenty years ago, is now known as suburbia.

7. Without a word she swept past her parents, mounted the stairs, slammed the door to her _____ and burst into tears.

8. Although a renowned surgeon, he was considered a _____ of the arts.

9. Hitler believed that the _____ would be sufficient to bring England to its knees and to surrender.

10. Some historians consider the Bay of Pigs _____ and the Cuban missile as the high and low points of President Kennedy's dealings with Cuba.

EXERCISE B

BE A VERBAL GOURMET

Directions: For each of the following phrases or sentences (a) give the original language of the italicized word and (b) provide a meaning according to context.

Example:
... *bivouacked* against the side of the mountain.
(a) German
(b) an encampment with little or no shelter.

1. Hemingway, an *aficionado* of bull fights.....

   (a)

   (b)

2. ... wore his borrowed *cummerbund.*

   (a)

   (b)

3. ... the impending threat of the breaking ice *floe.*

   (a)

   (b)

4. a massive *hegira* from the volcanic area ...

   (a)

   (b)

5. . . . approached the *hustings* as people applauded.

(a)

(b)

6. The *kibitzer* was unpopular with the gamblers.

(a)

(b)

7. Read the *scenario* before the performance.

(a)

(b)

8. An understanding of Bismark, the man, leads to a better knowledge of Germany's *zeitgeist* at the turn of the century.

(a)

(b)

9. The *intelligentsia*, especially artists, poets and novelists, have often suffered under the policies of the Russian government.

(a)

(b)

10. . . . his *ghoulish* and morbid features.

(a)

(b)

11. . . . awaited Hitler's final *fiat* before marching into Poland.

(a)

(b)

12. *The Old Man and the Sea* has been called by some a modern American *saga.*

    (a)

    (b)

13. The congressman travelled *incognito* in order to learn their candid opinions.

    (a)

    (b)

14. Cheating on an examination is *verboten.*

    (a)

    (b)

15. Her *gauche* mannerisms showed her complete ignorance of etiquette.

    (a)

    (b)

16. The company required a *dossier* of her qualifications and references.

    (a)

    (b)

17. The starlet's *hauteur* was very annoying.

    (a)

    (b)

18. Many of Poe's short stories are masterpieces of *macabre* writing.

    (a)

    (b)

19. Kicking the first-base bag became a *fetish* for the right fielder.

    (a)

    (b)

20. Adolf Eichmann was convicted of masterminding the *pogrom* under Hitler.

    (a)

    (b)

SUPPLEMENTARY EXERCISE

Some of our college courses have retained many foreign words in their vocabularies; frequently this is so because this art or science had its beginnings or reached its peak in a certain country. Thus we find many German words in our modern technologies, many Italian in the field of music, and many French in the fine arts.

MUSIC APPRECIATION AND ITALIAN

If you are interested in good music or if you are taking a course in Music Appreciation, a knowledge of the following Italian words is considered necessary for an adequate understanding of the subject. Answer each of the following statements. You may use your dictionary.

1. If "mezzo" means "half," than a mezzo-soprano would probably sing:
   (a) higher than soprano
   (b) lower than a contralto
   (c) between a soprano and a contralto
   (d) none of the above

2. Which of the following does not properly belong with the rest of the group?
   (a) contralto
   (b) mezzo-soprano
   (c) soprano
   (d) baritone

3. If the ensemble were to sing without the aid of any musical instrument, the cast would necessarily be singing:
   (a) a cappella
   (b) an aria
   (c) a concerto
   (d) a scenario

4. Which would you most likely hear at an opera?
   (a) an aria
   (b) a cantata
   (c) a concerto
   (d) a sonata

5. Upon entering a theatre to witness an opera you would expect to receive:
   (a) an allegretto
   (b) a falsetto
   (c) a libretto
   (d) a serenata

6. The finale would probably be conducted by the:
   (a) improvvisatore
   (b) maestro
   (c) prima donna
   (d) virtuoso

7. Which of the following would probably have the leading role at a symphony?
   (a) maestro
   (b) prima donna
   (c) virtuoso
   (d) voce di testa

8. The opposite of pianissimo is:
   (a) adagio
   (b) forte
   (c) falsetto
   (d) obligato

9. Which of the following directional words does not belong with the others?
   (a) accelerando
   (b) adagio
   (c) andante
   (d) largo

10. Obbligato, pizzicato and stoccato are all:
    (a) directional acting words
    (b) types of musical compositions
    (c) words directing a style of playing
    (d) vocal directional words

LESSON 4

WHAT DID
HE SAY?

FOREIGN EXPRESSIONS

Frequently during a student's studies he is confronted with foreign phrases. A poet may be criticized for his *belles lettres*; an author may bemoan the *succès d'estime* of his novel; a professor may fault your *non sequitur* arguments in a term paper; our ambassador to Russia may be branded *persona non grata*; *et cetera.* Why don't people speak and write plain English?

The reasons for using foreign expressions are quite simple. The alien words should express the exact thoughts of the speaker or writer, thoughts which for various reasons could not be said better in English. Often the expressions are drawn from various quotes; *e.g.: carpe diem* (Horace, "enjoy today" *Ars Poetica*), *jacta est alea* (Caesar when crossing the Rubicon, "the die is cast"); common sayings: *mirabile dictu* (Cicero, "wonderful to relate"); references: *annus mirabilis* ("year of wonders," especially 1666, the year of the London fire and the Black Plague); and special terminologies, like law: *habeas corpus* (you should have the body), *ex post facto* (after the event).

Such expressions add to the tone, clarity and the significant meaning of a sentence or paragraph. It should be flattering to the student to feel that a professor or an author assumes that his education embraces a keener knowledge of the niceties of language. Yet some students not only do not take the time to look up these foreign phrases in their dictionaries, but they do not even attempt to read them.

EXERCISE A

WHAT'S IN A PHRASE!

Following is a list of some foreign expressions with their literal meanings. You are to study them and then complete each of the following sentences by inserting the apropos expression. After this, return to the list and give a common meaning for each expression.

Phrase	Language	Literal Meaning	Common Meaning
coup d'état	French	stroke of state	
cul de sac	French	bottom of the sack	
deus ex machina	Latin	god from a machine	
ex officio	Latin	from the office	
faux pas	French	false step	
hoi polloi	Greek	the people	
nom de plume	French	name of the pen	
sine qua non	Latin	without which not	
sub rosa	Latin	under the rose	
vis-à-vis	French	face to face	

1. The president of the Student Government Association was _____ chairman of the Student Cultural Committee.

2. The military Greek junta was successful in its bloodless _____ which deposed the king.

3. The campaign speeches of the politician placed him in an unfavorable _____ when he began his term of office.

4. Samuel Clemens' _____ was Mark Twain.

5. The play's _____ ending resolved the problem but was a very unrealistic solution.

6. In many underdeveloped nations the communists have appealed to (the) _____ for their support and strength.

7. North Vietnam originally stated that the unconditional halting of the bombing was a _____ condition before any peace talks could be held.

8. The French ambassador committed a _____ when he preceded his prime minister into the National Assembly.

9. When confronted _____ his victim, the bold, audacious attacker became timid and cowardly.

10. The first meetings with the North Vietnamese were held _____, weeks before President Johnson's statement to the public.

EXERCISE B

SHOW YOUR KNOWLEDGE!

Here are some more common foreign phrases with which you should be familiar. For the most part the first group concerns the social sciences, such as history and sociology. The second are more literature oriented and you are more likely to find them in your general reading. With the aid of your dictionary, (a) give the most recent language from which the word has been borrowed and then (b) copy one of its modern meanings. *N.B.* If you are unable to locate a phrase then you can assume that your dictionary considers it still to be foreign and not common.

GROUP I—SOCIAL SCIENCES

Phrase	*Language*	*Meaning*
1. ad hoc		
2. aide de camp		
3. a priori		
4. enfant terrible		
5. esprit de corps		
6. ex cathedra		
7. fait accompli		
8. homo sapiens		
9. in loco parentis		
10. laissez-faire		
11. lebensraum		
12. persona non grata		
13. petit bourgeois		
14. quid pro quo		
15. zeitgeist		

GROUP II—LITERARY PHRASES

Phrase	*Language*	*Meaning*
1. affaire d'honneur		
2. annus mirabilis		
3. belles lettres		
4. bon vivant		
5. carte blanche		
6. chef-d'oeuvre		

31

Phrase	Language	Meaning

7. comme il faut
8. coup de grâce
9. in toto
10. pièce de résistance
11. savoir faire
12. succès d'estime
13. sui generis
14. tour de force
15. Weltanschauung

SUPPLEMENTARY EXERCISE

Since our legal system is based on the Roman Law, much of the terminology used in our courts retains its Latin origin. Although the following words in italics are fairly common, you may use your dictionary in answering the questions.

What does the judge mean when he:

1. orders a *non sequitur* statement to be struck from the records?
2. issues a writ of *habeas corpus* to the suspected thief's lawyer?
3. *subpoenas* all interested parties in the case?
4. in this instance questions the *modus operandi* of the district attorney's office?
5. rules that the contract was *ab initio* null and void?
6. orders the jury to consider the entire *corpus delecti* before reaching a decision?
7. releases a criminal on the inadmissibility of *ex post facto* laws?
8. requests the aid of an *amicus curiae* in locating a precedent?
9. judges the defendent incapable of standing trial because of his *non compos mentis*?
10. strongly advises the parties that he considers the case *res judicata*?

LESSON 5
NOT ALL
THAT BAD

USING CONTEXTUAL CLUES
FOR DERIVING THE
KNOWLEDGE OF WORDS

Reading a dictionary may intrigue some people, but for the average student even reading *with* a dictionary may prove to be too time consuming. Besides, a word in isolation frequently does not convey a complete thought. It depends on its use in the context (other words, phrases, clauses, or sentences surrounding it). Let us examine a few methods of applying contextual clues.

1. Deductive Reasoning
With Contextual Clues

Example:

>   He retired to his *château* in the country far from the crowded and bustling life of the city.

   Assuming *château* is an unfamiliar word, let us look at the various clues provided. Retired to what? Obviously, some place. Where? "In the country." But what kind of place? It must be the opposite of a "crowded and bustling life." Thus you should be able to assume, deduce, that a *château* is some type of a peaceful country home. Would you have to look this "unfamiliar" word up in a dictionary? Probably not, yet more than likely you have now added a new word to your vocabulary.

2. Parallel Construction Clues

Example:

Be thou *anathema;* go and never more return!

Assuming *anathema* is an unfamiliar word, note the clause which follows and the exclamation mark at the end. Someone is being told in very harsh language to "get out." It would appear then that this is a sufficient meaning for your reading vocabulary. If a more precise understanding of the word is wanted, then you should check the dictionary.

3. Contrasting Clues

Example:

Take back your cheap, imitation jewels. You cannot *foist* them on me.

The contrast between "back" and "on" in the two sentences should lead you to the definition of *foist*—to force a person to accept something. Again, your reading vocabulary can be satisfied with such a meaning, but before employing this or a similarly learned word check your dictionary for its refinements of meanings.

4. Appositive Clues

Example:

The pleasing sound effects of prose depend partly on the avoidance of *cacophony,* harsh sounds, and partly on combinations of sounds, stresses, *etc.* which somehow appeal to our inner sense of hearing.

In the above sentence the appositive phrase, "harsh sounds," actually defines the term *cacophony.* Since most appositives set off by commas, limit, qualify, or add meaning, they are usually easily recognized.

5. Combination of Contextual Clues

Example:

The province was famous for its export of zinc oxide, or *tutuja* (from the Persian word *Dud* meaning "smoke"), a medication used especially for the eyes.

Here the author provides his readers with various contextual aids to help them understand a little known term which is important to his discussion of his "Metallurgical Expedition through the Persian Desert." (*Science,* March, 1968). First, he defines *tutuja,* "zinc oxide"; next he presents some of its etymology which helps to describe it; and lastly, he tells briefly what it is used for.

Most textbook authors attempt to know the level as well as the type of students for whom they are writing. Not only does a good writer define his terminology but he also seriously tries to provide his readers with as many contextual aids as possible so that they can more readily understand what his ideas are. An author deals in thoughts and he cannot presume to be very successful if he is overly erudite, requiring his readers to look up every tenth word in a dictionary.

EXERCISE A

FROM YOUR TEXT

All of the following statements have been drawn from college English textbooks. You are to write a meaning for each of the italicized words or phrases, using the contextual clues and your dictionary wherever necessary. Brief references are given in parenthesis.

1. Like Chaucer, Shakespeare, Milton, and Browning, Gray was a poet *par excellence*. ("Gray," *College Survey of English Literature*, Witherspoon, *et al*.)
2. We find ourselves plunged into the situation *in media res*; whatever background we are to receive is given to us incidentally . . . ("Ballads," *ibid*.).
3. Your real research begins with your efforts to find the right articles in periodicals, books and articles that have appeared since the latest bibliography was compiled. For both objectives the periodical *indexes* are indispensable. ("Documented Essays," *Contemporary Rhetoric*, Daniel.)
4. Short, choppy sentences at times can produce an effective tone, an emphatic, *staccato* effect. ("Style," *Essentials of Grammar and Style*, McCollum.)
5. Essentially, the protagonist in *picaresque* comedy (such as Ben Johnson's *The Alchemist*) is the underdog rogue who lives by outwitting his more prosperous but less astute neighbors. ("Comedy," *An Introduction to Literature,* Barnet, Berman and Burto.)
6. Aristotle has some obscure comments on *catharsis*, which are often interpreted as saying that tragedy arouses in us both pity and fear and then purges us of these emotions. ("Tragedy," *ibid*.)
7. With this speech the major issue is clearly settled and the *denouement* (literally, "unknotting") begins. ("Drama," *Interpreting Literature*, Knickerbocker and Reninger.)
8. Here (*An Enemy of the People*) one may feel that Ibsen has resorted to *deus ex machina,* for when the major reveals the contents of Mr. Kiil's will, we have a-rigged ending. ("Drama," *ibid*.)

9. The writer seeks "precision with elegance," the *mot juste* from a fairly large vocabulary and embeds it in an elegant pattern of word-order and clause interrelationship. ("Looking at English in Use," *The Use of English*, Quirk.)

10. It is in fact by analogy that many new words come into use, whether they are *portmanteaus,* like "brunch" (breakfast and lunch) . . . ("Words, Words, Words," *ibid.*)

EXERCISE B

MORE OF THE SAME

Here are some examples of how authors of college texts use contextual aid to clarify foreign words or phrases. You are to write a meaning for each of the italicized words or phrases. Again, for your information, brief references are provided.

GROUP A—THE FINE ARTS

1. The media are similar except that *collage,* as the name implies (the French verb, "coller" means to paste) calls for the gluing of materials to a surface. ("Painting," *Art as Image and Idea*, Feldman.)
2. The principal difficulty of nineteenth century *trompe-l'oeil*, or magicrealist art, lay in its lack of humanistic ambition. ("The Styles of Art," *ibid.*)
3. Yet whether historically the industrial arts preceded or came *pari passu* with the fine arts, analytically there is a distinction to be made. ("Arts and Civilization," *Arts and the Man*, Edman.)
4. In some operas, especially those of Wagner, a device known as *leitmotif* is employed. It is a theme used recurrently throughout to represent a character, an objective, or a situation. ("Opera," *Introduction to Music*, Miller.)
5. The recapitulation may be a *da capo aria* or it may be a modification of a main section of a musical composition. ("Musical Structure," *ibid.*)

GROUP B—THE SOCIAL SCIENCES

6. Closest to such sources are the "*Synoptic Gospels*," the New Testament books of Mark, Luke, and Matthew so called because they take the same general view. ("Christianity," *History of Civilization*, Brinton, *et al.*)
7. The characteristic style of the Enlightenment of the seventeenth century, which flourished in the France of Louis XIV, is often known as *l'esprit classique.* ("The Age of the Enlightenment," *ibid.*)
8. Although we can now perceive ourselves as the species, *Homo sapiens* . . . we find it disconcerting to be observed dispassionately as a colony of ants. ("Sociology and Science," *Man Among Men*, Mead and Mead.)

9. Most civilized as well as most primitive family groups are *exogamous* in keeping with the general taboo against incest, but sometimes the restriction goes beyond the immediate family. ("Culture," *ibid*.)

10. Under the Presidential Succession Act of 1947, if the President dies, and there is no Vice-President, the order of presidential succession puts the Speaker first in line, next the then acting president *pro tempore* of the Senate, ... ("Legislative Structure and Organization," *Dynamics of Democratic Government*, Roche and Stedman, Jr.).

11. The *entrepreneur*, the captain of industry, is the greatest engineer of industrial progress, for he directs the efficient functioning of labor and capital. ("Early American Economists, *The Evolution of Economic Thought*, Oser.)

12. Thinking built around personal needs is called *autistic* thinking, from the Greek root *autos*, meaning self. ("Thinking," *Introduction to Psychology*, Hilgard.)

13. We may classify drives into three groups: *visceral* drives (based on organic needs like those for food and water), activity drives (based on the need to use our muscles) ... ("Physiological Background of Motivation," *ibid*.)

GROUP C—MATHEMATICS AND THE NATURAL SCIENCES

14. If, by using the basic assumptions, a logical argument, or proof, is produced which shows that a general statement is true, the statement is called a *theorem*, or proposition ... ("Modern Mathematical Reasoning," *Elementary Concepts of Modern Mathematics*, Dinkines.)

15. A variable like the flip of a coin, which must show one of two outcomes in a single observation, is called a *dichotomous* variable. ("Decision Making and Risk," *Statistics on Intuitive Approach*, Weinberg and Schumaker.)

16. Two numbers may be compared in size by dividing one by the other. The quotient thus obtained is called the *ratio* of one number to the other. ("Ration, Proportion, and Variation," *College Algebra for Freshmen*, Fuller.)

17. Linnaeus gave us the Binomial System of naming organisms, which since the name in each case was in Latin, meant that the same organism would go by the same name in all parts of the world in scientific writings. His *Systema Natura* ... is regarded as the beginning of present-day *taxonomy*. ("Classification," *Biology*, Johnson, *et al.*)

18. The nonmetals fluorine, chlorine, bromine, and iodine are known as *halogens*, a name derived from the Latin word meaning "salt former." ("Chemical Properties," *Fundamentals of General Chemistry*, Sorum.)

19. Microscopic organisms, such as molds and bacteria, in the absence of oxygen, change leaves, fruit, and wood on or in the soil into the dark organic substance known as *humus*. ("Soils," *Principles of Geology*, Gilluly, *et al*.)

20. Strictly speaking the rainbow is not a perfect *spectrum*, since there is overlapping of the colors. ("Colors," Physics, *The Story of Energy*, Brown and Schwachtgen.)

SUPPLEMENTARY EXERCISE

Frequently the travel industry, in its advertisements, uses words which appear strange and foreign to the average reader. This is purposely done. First, they are eye-catchers, for if they are foreign, they have to be printed in a different type of print, italics. Secondly, they add a sense of mystique, enchantment, and sometimes intrigue. To help get the message across contextual clues are usually provided. Define the italicized words. Some may not be listed in your dictionary. For your information the sources of the advertisements are given.

1. Chanel-dressed hostesses wine and dine you to lively *bouzouki* (in stereo, of course). (Olympic Airlines.)
2. Stretch out in a hot spring where fierce *samurai* came hundreds of years ago to soothe their battle scars. (Japan Air Lines.)
3. Luxury is the Epicurean pleasure of a scrumptious dinner, cooked by masters of the art and served with *élan* by waiters who care. (Chandris Lines.)
4. We'll have a *lei* greeting awaiting you, plucked from the island by Hawaiian hands. (United Air Lines.)
5. Wherever you rove you can explore memorials of the romantic and cultured past giving you a feeling of *gemütlichkeit* in our busy and modern times. (German Democratic Republic Tourist Bureau.)
6. They sense when you'd rather grope for ideas than reach for *petit fours,* and when you'd welcome a few hours of rest more than a cocktail. (British Overseas Airways Corporation.)
7. Picture yourself in a silk shop in Madras where the proprietor is showing your wife a few floor-length *saris.* (Air India.)
8. The legacy flourishes still: the *haute cuisine* and the complimentary wine, the elegant Grand Salon, and the quiet luxury of her decor. (Paquet French Lines.)
9. You'll be served by a charming Polynesian hostess clad in a flowered *pareu.* (UTA French Airlines.)
10. The variety of accommodations ranges from authentic elegant *haciendas* in the wild country to hi-rise resort hotels overlooking the Pacific. (American Express.)

UNIT II

LESSON 6

WHAT'S IN
IT FOR ME?

*LOCATING INFORMATION
IN A DICTIONARY*

A dictionary is not the authority on words; rather it is a record of the acceptable literary usages of words. English is a living language, and as such it is in a constant state of flux. A lexicographer (writer of a dictionary) does not legislate for or against such changes as "slo" and "thru" for *slow* and *through*, or "if I was" in favor of *"if I were."* He must resign himself to his status as the recorder of the preferred educated spoken and written words.

Although many students carry a pocket-size dictionary with them, they must realize that it is abridged and probably does not contain all the information they will need for writing term reports or understanding specific terminologies. *Webster's New World Dictionary* (Popular Library: New York, 1959), one of the best in this category, contains approximately 50,000 entries, whereas most standard dictionaries have between 130,000 to 150,000 entries. As a college student, indeed, as an educated person, you should own and know how to use a collegiate dictionary. The five most widely used collegiate dictionaries are:

Webster's Seventh New Collegiate Dictionary (NCD), G. and C. Merriam Co.:
 Springfield, Mass., 1965.
American College Dictionary (ACD), Random House: New York, 1966.
Webster's New World Dictionary (NWD), World Publishing Co.: Cleveland, Ohio,
 1966.
Funk and Wagnalls Standard College Dictionary (SCD), Harcourt, Brace and
 World: New York, 1963.
Random House Dictionary of the English Language: College Edition: (RHDC),
 Random House: New York, 1968.

The chart on the following pages presents a comparison of the above standard collegiate dictionaries.

A Comparison of the Five Standard Collegiate Dictionaries

	Webster's Seventh New Collegiate Dictionary (NCD)	American College Dictionary (ACD)	Webster's New World Dictionary (NWD)	Funk & Wagnall's Standard College Dictionary (SCD)	Random House Dictionary: College Ed. (RHDC)
Latest Publication Date	1965	1966	1966	1963	1968
Presentation of Material	"Explanatory Notes" Intro. Sect.	"Explanatory Notes" Intro. Sect.	"Guide to the Use of the Dictionary" Intro. Sect.	"Plan of this Dictionary" Intro. Sect.	"Guide to the Dictionary" Intro. Sect.
Scientific and Technical Meanings	After general definitions	Usually under specialized	After general definitions	According to frequency of use	Frequency of use
Order of Definitions	Meanings in historical order of development	Central meaning and/or figurative, specialized, general, rare	Meanings in historical order of development	Frequency of use	Most common part of speech first, then frequency of use
Discussion of Pronunciation	"Guide to Pronunciation" Intro. Sect.	"Preface"	Intro. Section	"Plan"—Intro. Sect.	Article, "Pronunciation of English, "Guide II"
Inflectional Forms	Only irregular forms given	All irregular forms plus those which might cause confusion	Irregular or those offering difficulty in spelling or pronunciation	Irregular plus those causing any difficulty	All not formed by simple addition of regular endings; e.g., s, es, ed, ing
Location of Etymology	After part of speech	After definitions	After definitions	After part of speech	After definitions
Restrictive Labels Used	Time (e.g.; obsolete) Style (e.g.; slang) and Region (e.g.; dialect)	Time, Style, Region (e.g.; psy.)	Only: Colloquial, Slang, Obsolete, Archaic, Poetic, Dialect, British	Time, Region, Style, Subject and Foreign Language (e.g.; German)	Region, Time, Subject, and Level of Usage (Style)

44

	(NCD)	(ACD)	(NWD)	(SCD)	(RHDC)
Use of Synonyms	In paragraph following relevant entries; others cross referenced	At the end of relevant entries; cross referenced	In paragraph following an entry considered basic to its group; others are cross referenced	At the end of relevant entries in paragraph form, others cross referenced	At the end of many entries, others cross referenced
Use of Antonyms	None given	Some—following relevant synonyms	None given	Limited antonyms given—usually derivations	Some—usually in relation to the synonym of an entry
Homographs	Always listed and numbered	Always listed separately	When obviously different words, listed separately	Always listed and numbered	Always listed and numbered
Foreign Expressions	Body—no distinction between foreign and Anglicized	Body—those not completely considered English, identified by foreign language label before definition	Body—those not considered completely English, preceded by double dagger (‡)	Body—those not considered completely English, identified by foreign language label in italics before definition	Body—those not considered completely English, italicized
Location of Abbreviation	Appendix	Body	Body	Body	Body
Biographical Information	Appendix	Body	Body	Body	Body
Place Names and Geographic Formations	Appendix	Body	Body	Body	Body
Common First Names	Appendix	None Given	Body	Appendix	Appendix
Colleges and Universities	Appendix—U.S. and Canada; separate lists	Appendix—Just U.S.	Supplement—U.S. & Canada	Appendix—U.S. and Canada; separate lists	Appendix—U.S. and Canada; separate lists
Arbitrary Symbols and Signs	Appendix	Appendix	Supplement	Appendix	Appendix

	(NCD)	(ACD)	(NWD)	(SCD)	(RHDC)
Rules of Orthography (Spelling)	Appendix "Spelling"	"Table of Common English Spellings" Preface	No rules discussed in "English Language," Intro. Section	"Table of English Spellings" Intro. Section	"Table of Common English Spellings," Intro. Section
Rules Governing Usage	Appendices under Special Headings	Appendix "A Guide to Usage"	Intro. Section	Appendices	"Usage . . . ," Intro. Section
Form of Address	Appendix	None	Supplement	"Correspondence" only—Appendix	None
Vocabulary of Rhymes	Appendix	None	None	None	None
Presentation of Illustrations	Ratio of reduction provided	Scaled—some sizes given	Scaled	Scaled, actual sizes of plants and animals given	Detailed and Scaled—actual sizes given
Table of Weights and Measures	Body—Under appropriate entries	Back Fly Leaf	Supplement	Back Fly Leaf	Back Fly Leaf
Special Articles	None Given	In Preface: Noteworthy—"Synonyms and Antonyms" and "Usage Level and Dialect Distribution"	"The English Language," Intro. Section	"Brief History of the English Language" "Regional Variations in American Pronunciation" "Canadian English" Intro. Section "Greek & Latin Elements in English" Appendix	"Indo-European Language Chart" Historical Sketch of the English Language," "Basic Manual of Style"

EXERCISE A

COMPOUND WORDS

The dictionary presents compounds (two or more words connected to make a single thought) in their acceptable forms. They may either be hyphenated (high-frequency), spelled as a single word (highfalutin'), as two words (high fidelity), or as a combination of these (ultrahigh frequency).

Give the preferred dictionary spelling of the following compound words.

1. avant + garde =

2. brain + washed =

3. coup + de + grâce =

4. digital + computer =

5. devil + may + care =

6. east + south + east =

7. feather + bedding =

8. laissez + faire =

9. living + wage =

10. mass + media =

11. no + man's + land =

12. par + excellence =

13. sixty + fourth =

14. tax + exempt =

15. tri + pod =

EXERCISE B

PRONUNCIATION KEYS

Immediately following a word entry is its pronunciation. Since diacritical marks are used to indicate various sounds, you should be familiar with them or at least, know how to use them. Many dictionaries provide a pronunciation key at the bottom of alternate entry pages. Every good dictionary has an introductory section explaining how it can be used to its fullest. Many students have never even seen this section. Have you? Check the word entry and the introductory sections to answer the following questions. Key words are in italics.

1. Why is a *macron* used in a pronunciation key?

2. What is a *breve*?

3. How does your dictionary distinguish *primary* from *secondary accent* marks?

4. How does an accent mark affect the word *abstract*?

5. In what kind of syllable would you find a *schwa*?

6. Underline the *digraphs* in the following words:
   (a) chide   (b) dearth   (c) sham

7. Why is it preferable to use *acute* accents in such words as *Benét, exposé, résumé*?

8. What is the purpose of the *diaeresis* in such words as *Laocoön* and *naïvete*?

9. What does the cedilla under the "c" in such words as *façade* and *garçon* indicate?

10. What is the purpose of the *tilde* over the "n" in such Spanish words as *cañon, mañana,* and *señorita*?

LESSON 7

A WHOLE BUNCH OF "ONYMS"

A. SYNONYMS

As we have already seen and will continue to observe in subsequent exercises, English has been blessed with an abundance of words derived from many languages, especially Latin, French and Greek. Thus we frequently have a choice among words. Synonyms, when used properly, enable us to express ourselves in a variety of ways, often with greater preciseness. The dictionary not only provides us with various meanings and synonyms of certain words, but it also frequently helps us to differentiate among these choices.

For example, after the abbreviation *Syn.* for the entry *cause*, The Webster's Seventh New Collegiate Dictionary (NCD) reads:

> *Cause, determinant, antecedent, reason, occasion* mean something that produces an effect. *Cause* applies to any event, circumstance, or condition or any combination of these that brings about a result; *determinant* applies to a cause that fixes the nature of what results as a product or an outcome; *antecedent* applies to that which has preceded and may therefore be in some degree responsible for what follows or derives or descends from it; *reason* applies to a traceable or explainable cause of a known effect; *occasion* applies to a particular time or situation at which underlying causes become effective.

When the dictionary indicates "Syn see . . ." it is directing us to one of these groups of discriminated synonyms.

B. ANTONYMS

An antonym is a word which conveys the opposite meaning of another word. *Backward* is an antonym for *forward.* Some dictionaries provide antonyms of certain words directly following their synonyms. For example, the SCD lists five synonyms and three antonyms for the entry, *terse:*

> syn.: concise, pithy, succinct, compendious and laconic.
> ant.: diffuse, prolix and wordy.

Antonyms which are formed regularly by the simple addition of a common prefix like *in* or *non* are usually not given in a dictionary. You will not find *inclement* nor *noncombatant* listed as antonyms for clement or combatant.

C. HOMONYMS

A homonym is a word like another in sound and usually in spelling but different in meaning.

Strictly speaking, there are two different kinds of homonyms: homographs (same writing) and homophones (same sound). The former are words which are spelled alike and have the same sound but have a different meaning. *Bear* a burden and catch a *bear;* having a *fair* complexion and a country *fair* are examples of homographs. Homophones, as the name implies, are words which sound alike but are different in spelling and in meaning. *Bare*-faced and transit *fare* are examples of homophones which correspond to the above homographs - *bear* and *fair*.

D. HETERONYMS

A word with the same spelling as another but which has a different pronunciation and meaning is called a heteronym (shed a *tear, tear* the paper). Heteronyms (other name) are listed as separate entries in the dictionary.

EXERCISE A

THE THREE H'S

Indicate by "A" for homograph, "B" for homophone or "C" for heteronym the relationship between each pair of italicized words in the following phrases.

1. six inch *bass,* sings first *bass* _____

2. *bore* a hole, *bore* no hard feelings _____

3. a *lead* pipeline, *lead* a trump card _____

4. in the *main,* clipped his *mane* _____

5. the *principal* speaker, the *principle* of the matter _____

6. *refuse* permission, littered with *refuse* _____

7. quit before you're *fired, fired* with envy _____

8. *tales* of yore, coat and *tails* _____

9. wait a *minute*! a *minute* particle _____

10. a *filing* cabinet, a rough *filing* before sanding _____

E. ACRONYMS

An acronym is a word formed from the first letter *or letters* of successive parts of words. Catchy acronyms play a large role in the commercializing of our American way of life. Government agencies (VISTA), organizations (CORE), companies (NABISCO), education (SEEK—Search for Education, Enlightenment and Knowledge), the military (WAC), and the television and movie industry (Man from U.N.C.L.E.) are especially fond of creating these new words.

51

EXERCISE B

WHAT DO THEY REALLY MEAN?

(1) These are some of the more noteworthy and representative acronyms. Give the complete title or derivation for each. (2) Since many are considered complete words, look in the body of the dictionary before referring to an Appendix of Abbreviations. (3) Some may not be located in a dictionary, but you should be able to figure out those for yourself.

1. co-ed

2. co-op

3. diazine

4. gestapo

5. jujitsu

6. laser

7. NASA

8. NATO

9. Nazi

10. okay

11. scuba

12. SEATO

13. TASS

14. UNESCO

15. WHO

SUPPLEMENTARY EXERCISE

MILITARY COINED ACRONYMS

1. AMVETS

2. AWOL

3. flak

4. GI

5. jeep

6. noncom

7. POW

8. radar

9. ROTC

10. SAC

11. Seabee

12. sonar

13. snafu

14. UFO

15. WAVE

LESSON 8

THE RITES
FOR RIGHT
SPELLING

VARIED SPELLING

Although the English that *we speak* is basically phonetic, approximately twenty per cent of our written language is non-phonetic. This is due to the large foreign word borrowings and to the great Vowel Shift of the sixteenth century wherein many long vowel sounds changed from their Latin to the modern $\bar{a}, \bar{e}, \bar{i}, \bar{o}$, and $\bar{u}$.

With good reason, English is considered one of the most difficult languages to spell. *Wait* and *weight* the *ways* before you *waste* your time. *Though* he had a *rough cough* he weathered *through* the *hiccough* attack. Isn't it about time someone tried to simplify the rules for spelling?

Almost seven hundred years ago, Fra Orrm tried. In proposing and writing in a system in which all consonants preceding short vowels were doubled, he succeeded in achieving one of the greatest *succès d' estime* of all times; yet, no one has given consideration to his work. John Cheke (c. 1550) advocated eliminating all final "e's," silent consonants and all needless letters. Thomas Smith in 1568 wanted to add eight more letters and accent marks over long vowels to distinguish them from the short ones. Fortunately for us and the English language none of these or other proposals ever received wide-spread acceptance. Samuel Johnson, through his dictionary (1755), became the first real authority on English spelling, for, although he advocated some changes and was criticized for being "rule-ridden," he did attempt to present the words in their most acceptable fashion.

Probably the most noted orthographic reformer was Noah Webster whose first dictionary appeared in 1789. Not only did he stress uniformity of spelling for reasons of clarity but also for patriotic reasons as this would necessitate the patronizing of U.S. printing houses and make for further independence from

Britain. Among other changes, he was responsible for (1) omitting, but with no apparent consistency, the double consonant; e.g., *jewellery* became *jewelry; waggon, wagon;* (2) dropping the final "k" after "ic" as in *magic* (k) and *public* (k); (3) reversing the letters "re" when it has the "er" sound as *center* for *centre* and *meter* for *metre;* and (4) dropping the "u" before "or" like in *color* for *colour* and *honor* for *honour.*

But there have been more recent advocates for a unified and simplified spelling system. Sir Isaac Pittman, one of the innovators of shorthand, devised, back in 1843, a phonetic system based on an alphabet of forty letters. Today many first and second graders are attempting to learn to read by a modern version of his theories called i/t/a. In 1906 Andrew Carnegie endowed a Simplified Spelling Board which, although affecting some good changes, ("catalog" for "catalogue," and "medieval" for "mediaeval"), was eventually "laftd to deth" for some of its "so cald rediculus creativs." George Bernard Shaw willed the royalties from *My Fair Lady* for research on spelling reforms. One modern system, Unifon, is attempting to eliminate our "old-fashioned" alphabet and substitute an entirely different set of symbols.

But man is a creature of habit, reluctant to change, and therefore it is highly improbable that spelling will be made easier in our lifetime. Try writing "tho," "thru," "nite," etc., on your term reports and your grades will probably be poorer. It is not a crime to have difficulty with spelling but it is the sign of an unlearned man to allow spelling mistakes to appear on any of his papers, especially if he has had the opportunity to do his writing at home or in the library where a dictionary is a handy reference.

EXERCISE A

VARIED SPELLINGS

Most standard collegiate dictionaries (NCD, NWD, SCD) will devote a section, either in the preface or appendix, to discuss the rules for spelling.

Part I: Circle the preferred American spelling for each of the following. You should be able to recognize them without the aid of your dictionary.

1. armor, armour
2. cigaret, cigarette
3. daemon, demon
4. dialog, dialogue
5. louver, louvre

6. nosey, nosy
7. offence, offense
8. plough, plow
9. theater, theatre
10. visor, vizor

Part II: Some of the following pairs of words are acceptable varied spellings; others are completely different words. Circle the number representing the varied spellings.

1. aesthetic, esthetic
2. council, counsel
3. draft, draught
4. fuse, fuze
5. gray, grey

6. minuet, minute
7. mold, mould
8. pray, prey
9. review, revue
10. sepulcher, sepulchre

EXERCISE B

ABBREVIATIONS

In formal and most ordinary writings, abbreviations are not permissible. There are, however, some standard exceptions with which you should be familiar. The NCD has no appendix devoted to abbreviations while the others ACD, NWD, SCD and RHDC include them within the main body of the dictionary.

Give the complete spelling and meaning for each of the following abbreviations and then indicate in what kind of writing you would likely find each. *N.B.* This latter information you will not locate in your dictionary; rather you will have to decide for yourself where it may be used.

Example:

ibid.—*ibidem*, in the same place; as a footnote in a book or on a term paper.

Abbreviation	*Meaning*	*Where Permissible*
1. Br		
2. C.O.D.		
3. etc.		
4. ESP		
5. fm.		
6. F.O.B.		
7. Gk.		
8. He		
9. IQ		
10. pct.		
11. Ph.D.		
12. pp.		
13. R.S.V.P.		
14. spp.		
15. wpm.		

SUPPLEMENTARY EXERCISE

After each of the following words, spelled in accordance with accepted British usage, write the preferred American form.

1. aluminium
2. barque
3. cheque
4. gaol
5. kerb

6. loch
7. lustre
8. pyjamas
9. programme
10. reflexion

LESSON 9

THE EXCEPTION PROVES THE RULE

INFLECTIONAL FORMS

Students often wonder why one must learn so many grammatical and orthographic (spelling) rules when they frequently are violated in everyday English usage. The rules are there supposedly because the exceptions occur fewer times than the regularities. As an eminent Greek professor once remarked, "The exception proves the rule," for if there were no exceptions, we would probably not need the rule.

When a word is transformed to show plurality, possession, conjugation or degree of comparison, that transformation is called inflection. To simplify, English has four kinds of inflection, namely:

   (a) Plurality—hats; dishes
   (b) Possession—hat's, hats'; dish's, dishes'
   (c) Conjugation—cleaned, cleaning; trapped, trapping
   (d) Comparison—quicker, quickest; more slowly, most slowly

But not all nouns form their plurals that easily; nor do all verbs form their past tense by adding "ed"; also some adjectives have irregular comparative and superlative forms. These irregularities tend to make the studying of English grammar difficult and sometimes boring.

Although each college student should own and know how to use a college handbook (*Modern English Handbook*:Prentice-Hall Inc., and the *Macmillan Handbook of English* are excellent choices) many times he will be able to locate the information he needs more readily in his desk dictionary. Irregularities are usually given after the entry in the main body, while the rules for forming plurals, inflectional endings, punctuation, capitalization, etc., are usually located in the addenda as in the NCD which has separate appendices for Spelling, Plurals, Punctuations, Compounds, Capitalization, and Italicization or in other dictionaries' "Guides to Usage."

EXERCISE A

WHICH SOUNDS BETTER?

Directions: Underline the correct inflectional form, using the dictionary where-ever necessary.

1. Many (analyses, analysises) must be accomplished before a theorem can be stated with any amount of certainty.
2. We hold these (beliefs, believes) to be self-evident: life, liberty and the pursuit of happiness.
3. The play tended to be monotonous due to the long, drawn out (soliloquies, soliloquys).
4. The Latin-American president's entourage seemed to be overly-staffed with (aide-de-camps, aides-de-camp).
5. It was the (worse, worst) hurricane to hit the eastern seaboard since the 1960's.
6. Sending flowers to the bereaved was the (least, lest) I could do.
7. (Politicing, Politicking) across the country was not his forte; therefore, he was not expected to win over many votes.
8. He was (refered, referred) to a guidance counselor to set up a (conference, conferrence) to discuss the matter.
9. The more the Marquis de Sade wrote, the (more bizarre, more bizarrer) his ideas became.
10. (Losened, Loosened) from bondage, the lioness darted into the jungle, forever free.

EXERCISE B

LOOK THEM UP!

Directions: Give the indicated form or forms for each of the following. Where more than one answer may be acceptable underline your dictionary's preferred choice. Your dictionary will provide inflectional forms considered uncommon.

1. plural of addendum

2. plural of genus

3. difference between stadiums and stadia

4. plural of criterion

5. present participle of dye

6. plural of fauna

7. plural of caucus

8. singular form of syntheses

9. comparative degree of the adjective little

10. singular of quanta

11. plural of mother-in-law

12. plural of nucleus

13. plural of radix

14. present participle of singe

15. plural of soprano

16. past tense of swing

17. plural of synopsis

18. past tense of traffic

19. present participle of use

20. superlative degree of unique

LESSON 10

SO WHAT
ELSE DOES
IT DO?

OTHER USES OF
THE DICTIONARY

A. Restrictive Labels

In Lesson 6 we pointed out that it is the duty of the lexicographer to record a word's usage and that English, as a living language, is constantly changing. Essentially then, whatever is said or is written is "correct" if it is understandable to those for whom it was meant.

However, some usages are more appropriate than others. Who determines this appropriateness? It is usually determined by the educational and cultural climate of the time, by its restrictive purpose in a given subject, and by its functional value in a particular area or situation. Thus dictionaries attempt to label or restrict the various usages and meanings of words.

The NWD has 30 different meanings for the noun *line*, six of which are reserved for usage in regard to bridge (the game), football, geography, mathematics, the military, and music. For the same entry the SCD gives 39 definitions, adding three nautical, one fine arts and two colloquial limitations. The ACD and the RHDC have 52 meanings for this word—new ones in the areas of baseball, electricity, law, politics, and television. The NCD has 13 major definitions. Three of these (an archaic form, one in bowling and another considered "chiefly British") are only found in this dictionary. All of these dictionaries examine some idiomatic phrases based on this single word, *e.g.,* hit the line, line of duty, *etc.*

Although different dictionaries may be at variance regarding the restrictive use of a given word, the prime criterion must be that the usage fits the situation as well as the location. A *poor boy,* a *hero,* a *hoagy,* and a *submarine* are all similar Italian loaf sandwiches, but unless you are in the right city, you might not get what you ordered. Do you know which city would go with which sandwich? Baltimore, Boston, New Orleans, New York? And then to wash down your lunch would you order pop, soda, or tonic?

If you are to use words appropriately and intelligently, you should know the various labels words may bear. The NCD uses restrictive labels of time (obs.), style (colloq.), and region (Brit.), while the other four standard college dictionaries also include subject labels (Anat., Baseball). The rules governing the proper usage of words are found in the NCD in addenda of spelling, plurals, punctuation, compounds, capitalization, and italicization. In the other dictionaries these are usually covered in their "Guides to Usage."

The answers to the above are:

Baltimore—hoagy and pop, Boston—submarine and tonic, New Orleans—poorboy and soda, New York—hero and soda.

A PRINTED ANSWER MAN—
THE DICTIONARY

How many of the following questions can you answer? Your dictionary can be of service for those of which you are not sure.

1. What is the difference between a *passed ball* in baseball and a *passed ball* in football? A football *tackle* and fishing *tackle*?
2. Where is a *perambulator* really a baby carriage?
3. What is a colloquial meaning of *jazzy*?
4. Who is expected to contribute to *Peter's Pence*?
5. Is *ain't* in your dictionary? If it is, when may it be used?
6. Who should be expected to know that *Rh* is the symbol for rhodium?
7. Where would you buy *petrol* for your *lorry*?
8. What is a *Rhodes* scholar?
9. What is a difference between the usage of the word *radical* in an Algebra course and a course in Western Civilization?
10. In its legal sense, is the phrase *"null and void"* considered repetitious?

B. Capitalization

Some words, like Indian and English, are always capitalized as they are considered to be proper nouns or adjectives; i.e., they always refer to a *particular* person, place, or thing. However, sometimes a word, derived from a proper noun, may have developed a more common meaning and therefore it should not be capitalized when used.

Directions: In this exercise give the meaning of the italicized word as it is used in the context and then give its alternate (capitalized or non-capitalized) meaning as found in your dictionary.

EXERCISE B

CAPITALIZING MAKES A DIFFERENCE

Example:
The athlete had *herculean* strength and stature.
(a) of extraordinary power, size, or difficulty
(b) characteristic of Hercules

1. The men of the *Kon-Tiki* were truly twentieth century *argonauts,* risking their lives to prove their scientific theories about the discovery of Polynesia.

   (a)

   (b)

2. Previously a confirmed bachelor, he was turned into a long-sought *benedict* by the beautiful girl.

   (a)

   (b)

3. The *elysian* retreat of his summer home enables him to settle his nerves.

   (a)

   (b)

4. He was more a philosophic *Epicurean* than just a believer in the slogan, "Eat, drink, and be merry for tomorrow we die."

   (a)

   (b)

5. Precisely at five-ten, cab drivers begin to jockey for positions to handle the nightly *exodus* from the city.

   (a)

   (b)

6. A good, hot cup of *java* has a way of soothing one's entire body.

   (a)

   (b)

7. During the spring recess, Fort Lauderdale becomes a *mecca* for thousands of college students.

   (a)

   (b)

8. The Oregon presidential primary loomed as a triumph of *gargantuan* proportions for both Richard M. Nixon and Eugene McCarthy.

   (a)

   (b)

9. The North's determination to preserve the *Union* was simply the form that the power drive now took. (E. Wilson, *Patriotic Gore*).

   (a)

   (b)

10. With the defeat of the Spanish *Armada,* England ruled the Seven Seas.

   (a)

   (b)

UNIT III

LESSON 11

A FEW CHOICE
MASTER KEYS

LATIN PREFIXES
PART I

We have already seen that a good collegiate dictionary contains between 130,000 (ACD) and 150,000 (SCD) words. Obviously we do not expect anyone interested in improving his vocabulary to sit down and read a dictionary. No, there is a more practical and quicker way. Learn to recognize affixes (prefixes and suffixes) and basic roots—elements of words which determine meanings. By adding various prefixes and/or suffixes to the Latin root *fer* meaning "to bring, to bear," we can form more than one hundred common words: refer, deferment, transferal, conference.

Addendum 1 contains a list of the common Latin prefixes. We do not expect you to memorize them; rather, it is more advantageous for you to be able to recognize them in familiar words and then to be able to apply this knowledge to unfamiliar words in which they are used. For example, if *ante* means "before" and *ced* is the Latin root for "go," then an antecedent is a noun that "goes before" its pronoun. If diluvian means "flood," then something which took place prior to Noah's time could be referred to as antediluvian.

71

EXERCISE A

"PROS AND CONS"

With your knowledge of the Latin prefixes you should be able to form antonyms (opposites) for each of the following words. Retain the same root.

Example:
predate—postdate

1. antebellum
2. deductive
3. exterior
4. immigrate
5. inferior
6. introvert
7. malignant
8. offensive
9. retrogress
10. suffix

EXERCISE B

MAKING SENSE WITH PREFIXES!

Based on your knowledge of the Latin prefixes, place a "T" for true after each true statement and an "F" for false after every false one. Italicized words are located on the prefix list.

1. An *unprecedented* murder trial dooms the defendant to conviction. _____

2. If *extracurricular* activities adversely affect your cumulative average, you would probably be well advised to discontinue them for awhile. _____

3. *Intracollegiate* sports are any athletic event between two or more colleges or universities. _____

4. The *attrition* rate of the freshman football team is of great concern to the head coach whose varsity has already had a deplorable season. _____

5. A word's *penultimate* accent occurs on the second last syllable of that word. _____

6. To *delineate* one's thoughts would be to attempt to express them accurately. _____

7. *Illicit* activities are of necessity *invalid* ones. _____

8. A *malevolent* remark is not intended to be taken as a *compliment*. _____

9. A *peninsula* is to the ocean as a bay is to a shoreline. _____

10. A *surrealist's abstract* is easily understood by a patron of the arts. _____

11. If an optometrist *occludes* a person's right eye, he should be better able to ascertain the vision of that eye. _____

12. An army chaplain may be considered a *noncombatant*. _____

13. The minister's tedious *circumlocutions* endeared him to his entire *congregation*. _____

14. The actor's *multifarious* talents led to his steady employment. _____

15. When the Southern States *seceded,* the United States became a stronger nation. _____

16. The speaker's *ambiguous* reply clarified his meaning. _____
17. There is an infinite number of *permutations* possible using the letters A, B, C and D. _____
18. The *postlude* came at the end of the concert. _____
19. *Transgressors* can be considered to be in error. _____
20. The student's *retrogression* was shown by his steady improvement in the skill. _____

SUPPLEMENTARY EXERCISE

One of the words in each of the following groups is not composed of a prefix plus other elements. Circle that word. Check Addendum 1 for the prefixes.

1. accede, allegation, alteration

2. cohesive, elocution, collonnade

3. comical, commodity, compensate

4. dilate, diplomatic, disheveled

5. ebony, educe, effervescence

6. ignite, ignoble, illustrate

7. imbibe, insoluble, irascible

8. occurrence, opposition, optimum

9. prologue, protract, purification

10. secede, seclude, sedative

LESSON 12

BLENDING
FOR EUPHONY

SOME FRENCH AND
GREEK EXAMPLES

Our Latin, French, and, to a lesser extent, our Greek linguistic forefathers were great euphonists; that is, they tried to make their words pleasing, if not to the minds and hearts, at least to the ears of their listeners. A Roman found *ad cumulare, cum respondere, ob pugnare,* etc. awkward and tongue twisters; therefore a system known as assimilation was developed. A prefix's final consonant was altered to match the initial consonant of the root. Thus he formed the words *accumulare* (accumulate), *correspondere* (correspond), and *oppugnare* (oppugn). Also, usually the final "m" in *com* became an "n" before a root beginning with the letter "t" as in *contribute* and *contrive*. However, some elements could be blended easily without the doubling of the root's initial consonant, and, in such cases, there was no need for assimilation. Consequently, we find words like *complain,* not copplain and *subservience,* not susservience.

EXERCISE A

A SPELLING HINT

Spell correctly the words formed by combining the indicated prefixes and the following elements. You are responsible for the meaning of each word.

Example:

ob + ponent = opponent

1. ad + nulment =

2. com + ponent =

3. dis + fident =

4. ex + feminacy =

5. in + com + rigible =

6. in + logical =

7. in + merse =

8. ob + cultism =

9. sub + cumb =

10. sub + dominant =

DOUBLING INITIAL CONSONANTS

One word in each of the following groups is misspelled. In the blank at the right spell that word correctly.

1. afiliate	aggregation	dissonance	_____
2. allude	digress	interogation	_____
3. contraband	retroactive	ilogical	_____
4. accelerate	coloquial	diffident	_____
5. innovate	pursuant	sufice	_____
6. eficacious	interracial	occidental	_____
7. dissatisfy	occasion	imure	_____
8. allegiance	ocult	unnerve	_____
9. abstemious	corelate	abhorrent	_____
10. efferent	suposition	subpoena	_____

SUPPLEMENTARY EXERCISE

Directions: With your knowledge of the prefix "con" and its various forms, you should be able to match the words in Column A with their meanings in Column B.

Column A	*Column B*
1. colloquy	A. abridgement
2. compatriot	B. assembly
3. competitor	C. dialogue
4. complacent	D. fellow countryman
5. commensurable	E. harmonizer
6. connote	F. irrevocable
7. convocation	G. mutual relationship
8. coordinator	H. proportionate
9. correlation	I. rival
10. corroborate	J. self-satisfied
	K. substantiate
	L. suggest

LESSON 13

UNUS, DUO, TRES

THE COMMON LATIN NUMERALS

We have seen how Latin prefixes affect the meanings of words as to degree (surrealist), direction (egress), negation (irrelevant), and time (antediluvian). There are also some Latin prefixes referring to number with which you should be familiar.

Let us demonstrate how a knowledge of the Latin prefixes "uni" and "bi" can enable you to derive new meanings from the word "lateral," (which is from the Latin *latus,* meaning "side").

(a) A _____ decision is completely one-sided.

(b) When two factions finally reach an accord, they have often arrived at a

_____ agreement.

Following is a list of common Latin numerals.

Latin	Meaning	Examples
semi	half, partly	semicolon, semicircle
uni	one, together	unity, uniform, unification
du, bi	two, twice	duplicate, bilingual
tri	three	triangle, trinomial
quadr	four	quadrilateral, quadrennium
quint, quincu	five	quintessence, quintuplet
sex	six	sextet, sextant
sept, septu	seven	September, septillion
oct	eight	octopus, octane
nove, nona	nine	novena, nonagon
dec (fr. G. deka)	ten	decimal, decade
cent	hundred	centenary, centipede
mill	thousand	milligram, mill tax

80

EXERCISE A

UNUS, DUO, TRES

Directions: Without the aid of your dictionary answer the following questions. Carefully study the words in the Examples Column, they are *not* the answers but they are clues. A prefix may be used more than once. Your answer may be of more than one word.

Example:

If man is a biped creature, then a quadruped should be (a four-footed creature).

1. An octave of _____ tones in the musical scale is a basic piano exercise.

2. Paperwork done in triplicate means that _____ copies are made.

3. In algebra we learned that a quadrinomial was an expression consisting of _____ terms.

4. The cessation of the infiltration was a unilateral action, since Israel took the action _____.

5. The Communists are noted for their continuous quinquenniums, which they maintain are necessary for their agricultural, cultural and economic reforms. A quinquennium is a _____ period.

6. Since the Roman year began with the Calends or the first of March, November was actually the _____ month of their calendar year.

7. Some schools are conducted on a trimester basis. This means that their academic year, exclusive of summer, consists of approximately _____ months.

8. When the Romans decided to decimate a percentage of barbarians, they planned to kill approximately every _____ man.

9. A Unitarian rejects the doctrine of the Trinity but believes in the _____ of God.

10. Septuagesima Sunday occurs _____ weeks before Easter.

EXERCISE B

SOME MORE COUNTING—WITH WORDS!

Directions: By referring to the list of Latin numerals, supply the words which will complete the following sentences. The Examples may provide clues. You may check your answers with your dictionary.

Example:

The U.N. delegate was a (*trilinguist*), speaking English, French, and Russian fluently.

1. Sports reporters often refer to a basketball team as a _____ _____.

2. Since Rome was founded over 2600 years ago, historians refer to it as being in its third _____.

3. As a person ages he may develop the need for glasses called _____ _____ to facilitate both near and far vision.

4. If a sexagenarian is a person in his sixties, then a man in his seventies is a _____.

5. If a parasitic animal has to depend for its existence on another organism, then we could classify an animal who depends only partly on another as a _____.

6. On July 4, 1976, the people of the United States will celebrate the second _____ of the signing of the Declaration of Independence.

7. A Roman _____ was in charge of a hundred soldiers.

8. If a meter, in the metric system, is approximately 39.37 inches, then .3937 inches is a _____ .

9. Many ancient philosophers considered air, earth, fire, and water to be the four essences of the world, reserving ether as the _____ , belonging solely to the heavenly bodies.

82

10. In statistics the term used for dividing the distribution of the sample into ten groups of equal frequencies is _____.

11. The chemical term for an element having a valence of six is _____ _____.

12. If the pact formed by Caesar, Pompey, and Crassus in 59 B.C. were correctly labeled a triumvirate, then a group of ten men who contract to work and rule together can possibly be termed a _____.

LESSON 14
DON'T FORGET
THE ENDING

COMMON SUFFIXES

A suffix is a syllable or syllables added to the ending of a word or root to form a new word. Although suffixes do alter—usually by degree—a word's or a root's meaning, their primary purpose is to change the functional use of the word or root. A word which functions as a certain part of speech such as the verb "tolerate" becomes a noun when "ance" or "ation" is added to its Latin root *toler*, an adjective with "able" or "ant," and an adverb with "ably" or "antly." Notice that in all of these variations the idea of "endurance" remains.

The suffix is an indication of a word's part of speech. The lists of suffixes located in Addendum 2 are separated into their parts of speech categories: noun-forming, adjective-forming, noun-adjective-forming, verb-forming, and adverb-forming. There are, of course, notable exceptions within these lists. "Ship," for instance, which is a noun-forming suffix is used as a verb-suffix in "People worship God." And "escent" may be used as either a noun or adjective in the word "adolescent." Another important value in knowing suffixes is that it can enable you to make fine distinctions. For example, a number of noun-forming suffixes like "ance" in compliance, "al" in radical, "ty" in deity, "ness" in appropriateness, are used to make abstract nouns, words naming mental concepts, conditions, or qualities. Some suffixes are used to form only concrete nouns; e.g., kibitzer, sociologist.

84

EXERCISE A

A. LESSON IN ABSTRACT THINKING

Directions: Form abstract nouns from the following phrases.

Example:

A state of being a serf—serfdom.

1. the state of being frustrated—
2. the quality of persevering in one's beliefs—
3. the quality of being concise—
4. one drafted into the armed forces—
5. an act of refusing—
6. the mental condition of being incorruptible—
7. the state of being despondent—
8. the feeling of being timid—
9. the condition of seceding from something—
10. the body of men that makes the law—

EXERCISE B

SUFFIX PUZZLERS

Part I. By changing the verb-forming suffixes make nouns and then insert them in the appropriate sentences.

a. associate   _____

b. activate   _____

c. strengthen   _____

d. justify   _____

e. antagonize   _____

1. The _____ was set so that the bomb would explode ten minutes after take-off.

2. As president of the Student Government _____, he was a member, ex officio, of the Student Faculty Advisory Committee.

3. Even the earliest Greek dramas had at least two main characters, the hero and his adversary, the _____.

4. Since the budget was defeated, every requisition must contain sufficient _____ for its immediate need.

5. The courage he exhibited was a bulwark and a _____ to the other men.

Part II. By adding, changing or deleting suffixes, make verbs from the following nouns and then insert them in the appropriate sentences.

a. summary   _____

b. deity   _____

c. insular   _____

d. coercion   _____

e. sympathy   _____

1. No one should be _____ to act against the dictates of his conscience.

2. Even before his murder Caesar had anticipated that his faithful followers would wish to _____ him and so he had a bust of himself already in the temple.

3. In conclusion you are to _____ the main points of your argument.

4. Although I _____ with his problems, I could not condone his actions.

5. In order to save on precious fuel, it is advantageous to _____ _____ the entire house.

Part III. By adding or changing suffixes make adjectives or adverbs from the following nouns or verbs and then insert them in the appropriate sentences.

a. concur   _____

b. judge   _____

c. origin   _____

d. verity   _____

e. tempest   _____

1. _____ he had intended to confess his guilt but the more he became involved the more difficult that became.

2. In order to create the greatest amount of confusion the two time-bombs were designed to explode _____.

3. Arthur Ashe's tennis victory was so resounding that the papers called it _____ triumph.

4. Your decision was a very wise and _____ one.

5. His _____ anger made him a very disagreeable person.

LESSON 15

THREE LITTLE BUT VERY IMPORTANT RULES

SUFFIXES IN SPELLING

Frequently a student, even in college, has spelling problems when confronted with adding suffixes to various roots or words. Here are a few general rules which may help you to spell better.

1. **Doubling the final consonant of the root.**
   A. If a suffix or inflectional form beginning with a vowel is added to a root or word ending with a consonant, which itself is preceded by a single vowel, that consonant is *doubled* providing its syllable is to be accented.

Examples:

concur, concurrent; refer, referred
   B. However, if the syllable is *not* to be accented then the consonant is not doubled.

Examples:

open, opening; refer, reference

2. **Words ending with "e."**
   A. If a suffix or inflectional form beginning with a vowel is added to a root or word ending with a silent "e," that letter is usually dropped.

Examples:

ensue, ensuing; fate, fatality
   B. However, if the root or word ends with a silent "e" preceded with a "c" (with an "s" sound) or a "g" (with a "j" sound) the "e" is usually retained to keep the soft sound of the "c" or "g."

Examples:

trace, traceable; advantage, advantageous

Exceptions:

trace, tracing; prejudice, prejudicial

    C. If a suffix or inflectional form beginning with a consonant is added to a root or word ending with "e," the "e" is usually retained.

Examples:

excite, excitement; tire, tireless

Exceptions:

argue, argument; true, truly

3. **Words ending with "y."**
    A. If a suffix or inflectional form is added to a word ending with a "*y*" which is preceded by a vowel, the "*y*" is retained.

Examples:

coy, coyness; deploy, deploying

    B. However, if the root or word ending with a "*y*" is preceded by a consonant, the "*y*" is usually changed to "i."

Examples:

faulty, faultiness; falsity, falsification

Exceptions:

hurry, hurried, hurrying

EXERCISE A

IMPROVING YOUR SPELLING

Directions: With your knowledge of the above rules spell the following correctly.

1. equip + ing =

2. bounty + ful =

3. notice + ably =

4. recur + ently =

5. colony + al =

6. deplete + ion =

7. incite + ment =

8. conjecture + ability =

9. concrete + ness =

10. manage + able =

11. decay + ed =

12. penny + less =

13. immense + ly =

14. relieve + able =

15. acquit + ance =

16. auspice + ous =

17. aspirate + or =

18. decrease + ingly =

19. submerge + ence =

20. foreclose + ure =

EXERCISE B

REVIEW OF PREFIXES AND SUFFIXES

By adding appropriate prefixes and suffixes replace the following phrases with a single word. Key words are underlined for your assistance. In some instances the *Latin root* is also provided. If necessary, check the Addenda.

1. the act of closing in a specified area _____

2. to give life to something _____

3. to strip a flower of its leaves (L.folium) _____

4. the act of coming between (L. ferire) two objects _____

5. a person who favors a political action in a reverse direction, extreme political rightism _____

6. to eliminate the separation (L. segregare) of the races _____

7. the moving (L. migrare) of a family from one country to another

    _____

8. the state of having your eternal destiny determined beforehand

    _____

9. following a surgical operation (adj.) _____

10. the artistic movement which attempts to portray the overly real

    _____

UNIT IV

LESSON 16

COMMON

LATIN ROOTS

*IT ALL STARTED WITH
EVE—THE SCIENCE
OF LINGUISTICS*

The study of language, linguistics, can be one of the most fascinating of the
sciences. What is it? What language did Adam and Eve speak? How are various
languages classified and why? How did our English language develop? Is
language really the *sine qua non* of civilization? These are just a few of the
questions we will consider in this Unit along with exercises based on some of the
more common Latin root elements.

Language is much more than a means of communication, for animals do this.
A bird's mating call and its warning cry are easily distinguishable. A dog's tail-
wagging frequently displays his temperament. You do not have to be a trained
specialist to extract the meaning of contentment, hunger, or anger from either
a cat's purring or a squirrel's chattering. These and other animal signs are
actually ideographic (representative) gestures and sounds, and cannot be considered languages because they lack the basic qualities of complexity, refinement,
and rationality which are characteristic only of human beings. Man, as we know
him, could not be such without language.

One of the earliest references to man's interest in linguistics is found in the
very first book of the Bible (Genesis, 2:19):

> And out of the ground the Lord God formed every beast and fowl of
> the air; and brought them unto Adam to see what he would call them: and
> whatsoever Adam called every living creature, that was the name thereof.

But language must be communicable, and so Adam had to convey his thoughts to

93

Eve and language was born. Let us look at a modern parody on the above Biblical quote and the supposed origin of the first language.

> ADAM: What makes you think you and I have anything in common?
> EVE: Well, for one thing, you're the only other animal that can talk!
> ADAM: That's how much you know! So can-so can-so can that flyer up there.
> EVE: Where?
> ADAM: In that tree.
> EVE: You mean that parrot? I didn't know parrots could talk!
> ADAM: Well, they can. Why do you call it a parrot?
> EVE: Because it looks like a parrot.
> . . .
>
> Adam: Sixth day, Adamtime. The naming goes recklessly on. I get no chance to name anything myself. The new creature names everything that comes along before I can get in a protest. And always on the same pretext— says it looks like the thing.[1]

Maybe Adam named his wife Eve, because her coming marked the end of a perfect day.

Before continuing our brief discussion of linguistics and, more specifically, the development of the English language, do the following exercises dealing with Latin roots that may be related to some of the more obvious communication skills. In this and the succeeding eight lessons the format will be to introduce the roots in the first column, their most general meanings in the middle, and examples of each in the last.

The Communications Skills

Root	Meaning	Examples
aud	hear	audile, audition, auditor
dic, dict	say	abdication, dictatorial, interdict
fac, fact, fec, fic	make	facsimile, factotum, infections, pacification
locu, loqu	talk	elocution, loquacious, soliloquy
scrib, script	write	proscribes, conscription, transcript
sed, sid	sit	insidious, preside, sedentary
spect, spic	see	perspicuous, retrospect, spectator
voc, vok	call	avocation, invoked, irrevocable

[1] Bock, Jerry and Sheldon Harnick, *The Apple Tree* (Random House: New York, 1966), pp. 9–10, 14.

EXERCISE A

SIMPLE COMPLETION

   By selecting a word from the "Examples" column, complete the following sentences. A word may be used only once; not all words are used.

1. The _____ for the advertising agency reported that the poor viewing of the program was not sufficiently promoting his sponsor's products.

2. When questioned by the attorney general, he repeatedly _____ _____the Fifth Amendment.

3. In many of Shakespeare's plays an actor will walk to the edge of the stage to deliver a _____.

4. Before a student may be accepted for matriculation, his high school _____ must be evaluated.

5. There can be no _____ of democratic rights for they are essential for true freedom.

6. A man's _____ may sometimes be more remunerative than his vocation.

7. The portrait was a very reasonable _____, especially since the artist had never seen the man.

8. Academic freedom is virtually under an_____in a
and
9. country which _____ what must or must not be taught in the classroom.

10. The _____existence of some of the Buddhist monks contributed to their longevity.

11. A _____ student is not guaranteed a good grade in a course in public speaking.

12. The scientists soon discovered that the _____ after-effects of the A-bomb were more pernicious than the actual bombing.

13. Some people hold that _____ of that territory is an absolute necessity before talks of disarmament can become a reality.

14. A child whose mental imagery is dependent more on his hearing or auditory capacities than on his visual or motor abilities is usually classified as an

    _____ .

15. There are two times in a man's life when he should not _____

    _____: when he can't afford it and when he can. (Twain, *Pudd'nhead Wilson*).

EXERCISE B

WORD BUILDING

Directions: Based on the roots, contextual clues, and your knowledge of affixes, complete the sentences. If necessary, check the answer in your dictionary.

1. In a state of shock after the accident, her replies to the police officer were almost _____. (*audire*—to hear)

2. It was an _____ speech which will be remembered for many years to come. (*loqui*—to speak)

3. The _____ at the bottom of the fish tank was a question of some concern to the biology professor. (*sedere*—to sit)

4. The president's decision not to run was not considered _____ _____ by other political leaders. (*vocare*—to call)

5. In retrospect the _____ of some editorial writers seemed to have been unnecessarily severe. (*dicere*—to say)

6. Running is considered the most _____ of all exercises. (*bene*—well + *facere*—to make)

7. Archeologists are still unearthing _____ of ancient Greek and Roman writers. (*scribere*—to write)

8. The _____ of the graduation speaker appealed very strongly to the emotions of the parents and guests. (*dicere*—to speak)

9. Because of her foolish actions, she made a _____ of herself at the party. (*spectare*—to look at)

10. A faculty is a power of the mind while _____ is the power to do anything easily and quickly. (*facere*—to do)

LESSON 17

LANGUAGE FAMILIES OF THE WORLD

THE CLASSIFICATION OF LANGUAGES

What was man's original language? This is a question which has baffled men for centuries. Herodotus (fifth Century B.C.) records the story of the Pharaoh, Psammetickos, determining that it was Phrygian. He isolated two newborn infants and required their nurses not to speak near or to them. After some months one child uttered a sound which appeared to be phonetically similar to the Phrygian word for bread, a necessity of life. Therefore, he stated, Phrygian must be man's original language. Early Christians, as well as many Jews for hundreds of years previously, believed that ancient Hebrew was the first language, for were not the Jews the chosen people, and had not God, Himself, talked with Abraham and Moses? The revival of Aristotelian philosophy in the thirteenth century and the recognition of semblances and dependences of Hebrew on earlier forms of the Semetic languages by eighteenth century scholars like Von Herder helped to dispell this theory. The philosopher Rousseau expounded the thought that primitive men, having a need for communication, merely invented one. Anthropologists, both contemporaries of Rousseau and modern, have continually sought for mankind's mother tongue but have found none. The Basque have contended that theirs is the original language since it seems to be the world's only "pure" one, not derived from any other. Theories we have; facts we have none.[1]

There are approximately 2,700 different languages, not counting myriads of dialects, spoken in the world today.[2] Certainly there must be some way of classifying them and determining the "mother tongues." One such is the Comparative

---

[1] Laird, Charlton, *The Miracle of Language* (Fawcett World Library: New York, 1957), pp. 23-24.
[2] Gray, Louis H., *Foundations of Language* (Macmillan: New York, 1939) quotes the French Academy's count of 2,796 different languages, p. 147.

Method developed in the nineteenth century. Similarities of languages, with systematic differences between them, are shown to have regular correspondences, or, in the case of the Indo-European languages, follow Grimm's Law for the various "sound shifts." An example of this is demonstrated in the initial Greek and Latin "p" sound developing into the corresponding "f", and sometimes "v" of the major Teutonic languages. For convenience, English script is used in the Grimm's Law for the initial "p" sounds.

Table A

Greek	Latin	Swedish	Danish	Dutch	German	English
pater	pater	fader	fader	vader	vater	father
platys	plattus	flat	flad	vlat	flach	flat
pous	pes	fot	fod	voet	fuss	foot
pleres	plenus	full	fuld	vol	voll	full

Thus you can see how a philologist can show that not only is there an affinity between the Teutonic tongues but also there must be some relationship among them and Latin and Greek as well. Carrying these principles further, linguistic scholars arrived at a fundamental language family for these and other similarly connected languages and labeled them Indo-European. The Comparative Method was scientifically applied to all the languages of the world and the general consensus was the following alphabetical classification of language-families.[3]

Table B

Alphabetical Classification of Language Families

1. Ainu—spoken by Caucasoid people of Japan
2. Australian and Papuan—spoken in Central Australia and New Guinea
3. Basque—spoken by a people in the Pyrenees mountain range of Northern Spain
4. Bantu—spoken by a people inhabiting south equatorial and southern Africa
5. Caucasian—spoken by a people residing in the Caucasus region between the Black and Caspian Seas.
6. Dravidian—spoken in southern India, West Pakistan, and Ceylon
7. Eskimo—American Indian (North and South America)
8. Hamito-Semitic—spoken in northern Africa and the Arabian Peninsula
9. Hottentot—spoken by the Bushman of southwestern Africa
10. Hyperborean—spoken by a people living in Siberia
11. Indo-European—spoken in most of Europe, Persia and most of India and Pakistan (English, French, German, Italian, Russian, etc.)

[3]Hughes, John P., *The Science of Language* (Random House: New York, 1964), pp. 51-9.

12. Japanese-Korean—spoken in most of Japan and Korea.
13. Mou-Khmer—spoken in southeast Asia, mainly Burma and Thailand
14. Polynesia—spoken in Malaya and many of the South Pacific islands
15. Sino-Tibetan—spoken in China and Tibet
16. Sudanese—spoken in equatorial Africa
17. Ural-Altaic—spoken by the Mongols, Turks, Finns, and Magyars of Hungary

The map on the following page indicates by the alphabetical classification number the location where the various language families are spoken today.

Before proceeding into a discussion of our particular language family tree, Indo-European, do the two vocabulary exercises which deal with the Latin roots pertaining to the parts of the body.

Biologically Speaking

Roots	Meaning	Examples
anim	spirit, mind, soul	animation, unanimous
capit, cipit	head, main	capitulate, precipitate
card, cord	heart	cordially, cardiogram
carn	flesh	carnivorous, incarnate
dent	tooth	dental, indentation
man, manu	hand	manual, manufacture
ocul	eye	oculist, binocular
ped	foot	pedestal, pedestrian

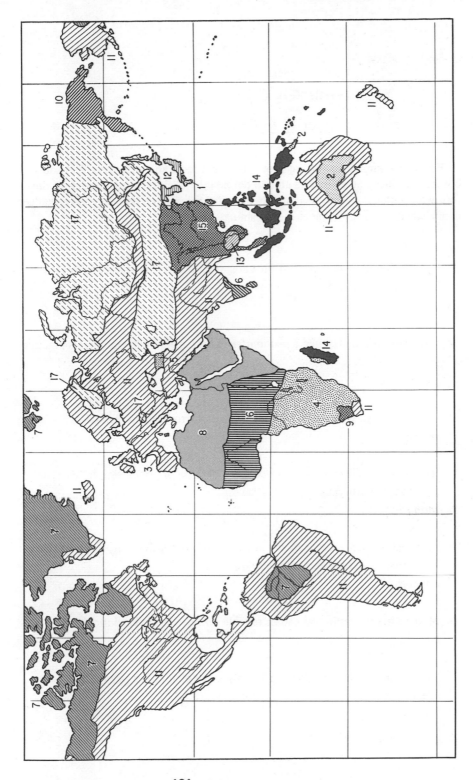

101

EXERCISE A

TRACE THE CLUES

From your knowledge of the above roots and roots and with the aid of some contextual clues you should be able to define the italicized words in each of the following sentences. *N.B.* Commonly accepted meanings today may have changed considerably from the original root meaning.

1. One of the most numerous of the categories of specially shaped leaves is that known as the *cordates*.
   cordate—

2. Each contestant attached a *pedometer* to his leg before beginning his practice run.
   pedometer—

3. The policeman was forced to bring the suspect to court in *manacles*.
   manacles—

4. The German officer wore a *monocle* not because of poor vision in his right eye, but rather because it was stylish.
   monocle—

5. Although neither evidenced any apparent love for each other, there was clearly no *animosity* between them either.
   animosity—

6. Modern fire power in war causes terrible *carnage* on the battlefield.
   carnage—

7. The Keystone View Company's Telebinocular examines a person for *binocularity*.
   binocularity—

8. For one fateful moment he stared into the *precipice* and then leaped to his doom.

   precipice—

9. Lack of serious thought and effort could seriously *impede* progress in racial relationships.

   impede—

10. Although the *concordat* between Pius XI and Mussolini divested the Church of its temporal powers in Italy, nevertheless, it also constituted the Vatican City as a sovereign power.

    concordat—

EXERCISE B

HOW IT BEGAN

With the aid of your dictionary show how the word origins contributed to the basic meaning of the word.

1. animadversion—a censorious remark—

2. capitation—a poll tax—

3. concordance—agreement—

4. carnal—worldly—

5. dentifrice—tooth paste—

6. manumit—free—

7. pusillanimous—cowardly—

8. impediment—hindrance—

9. emancipation—freedom from bondage—

10. recapitulate—summarize—

LESSON 18

ALL THIS FROM ONE TOWER

THE INDO-EUROPEAN FAMILY OF LANGUAGES

In 1786, Sir William Jones, British Chief Justice of Bengali, India, startled a learned society in London by expounding a linguistic theory showing that the religious language of the Hindus, Sanskrit, bore to Greek and Latin "a stranger affinity . . . than could possibly have been produced by accident; so strong, indeed, that no philosopher could examine all three without believing them to have sprung from some common source which, perhaps no longer exists.[1] For the next hundred years British and other European linguists exhaustively researched the similarities of Sanskrit to Greek, Latin, and to almost all the other languages of Europe. As we have already discussed, the culmination was Grimm's Law (1819) and the development of the Comparative Method for classifying languages, especially family branches of Indo-European.

But what did this do to the Biblical theory of an original language and the scriptural account of the resulting confusion after the tower of Babel incident? Some scholars felt that with a scientific demonstration of Sanskrit's relation to Greek, Latin, English, German, and Russian the "mother tongue" was found. But mid-nineteenth century linguists gradually dispelled this contention by showing that most of the original roots were found in words like *beech, birch, willow, dog, horse, bear,* and *wolf,* all native to north central Europe and not in words like *palm, olive, laurel, tiger,* and *leopard* which would have been common to the Tigris—Euphrates Valley of Persia, the so-called cradle of civilization. Thus we must conclude that neither Sanskrit nor its ancestor Indo-European (whatever that may have been) could have been the first language.[2]

[1] Hughes, John P., *The Science of Language* (Random House: New York, 1964), p. 51.
[2] Pei, Mario, *The Families of Words* (Harper & Row: New York, 1962), p. 5.

Some nineteenth and twentieth century linguists assumed that since the world's languages are traceable to seventeen family trees (see map in the preceding exercise), there must be seventeen prime languages. Tombetti, in 1905, attempted to prove the monogenesis, unity of origin, of all languages by noting certain common characteristics. Today, linguists are continuing to discover word-links among the various language families.[3]

But linguists can only go so far—because recorded languages only go so far! However, it seems logical to conclude that if the present 2,796 spoken languages can be traced to seventeen sources, these, in turn, should have had their ultimate origin in another earlier, and an actual prime language, pre-dating our great tower.

English is one of the Indo-European languages; in fact, in its modern form it is the last branch to be developed. On the following page is a diagram showing the *chronological* formation of the various main branches of the Indo-European languages.

One's Beliefs

Root	Meaning	Examples
cred	believe	credence, creed
fid	faith	infidelity, confidential
jug, junct	join	subjugate, injunction
ora	pray	oratory, oracle
ten, tin	hold	tenet, continence
viv, vit	live	vitalize, revival

[3]*ibid.*, p. 4.

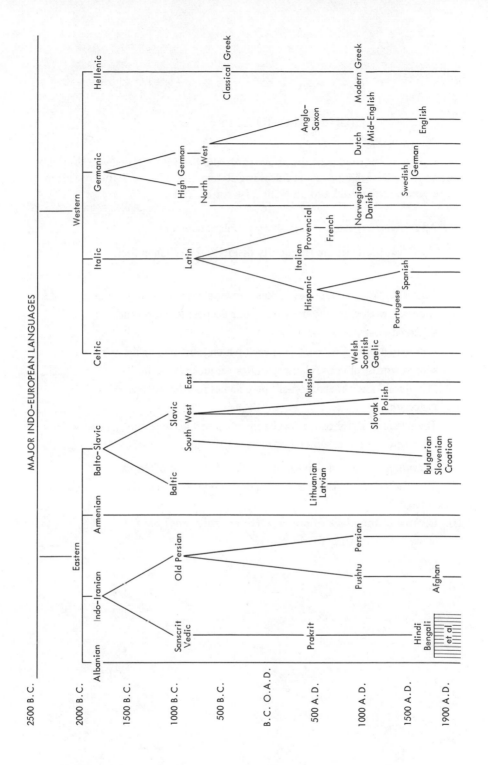

MAJOR INDO-EUROPEAN LANGUAGES

107

EXERCISE A

RIGHT OR WRONG?

From your knowledge of the above roots and previous affixes, you should be able to judge the validity of the following statements. Place a *T* for true after those you consider valid and an *F* for false for the others.

1. An *incredulous* statement is always a false statement. _____

2. *Credulous* students are frequently disinclined to change their ideas. _____

3. John's *perfidious* character makes him totally trustworthy. _____

4. A person with whom you entrust your deepest secrets could be called your *confidant.* _____

5. A *conjunction* is that part of speech which joins two or more similar words, phrases, clauses, and/or sentences together. _____

6. "Conjugal" and "matrimonial" may sometimes be used as synonyms. _____

7. The *oracle* at Delphos was probably so-named because she supposedly acted as a priestess between the gods and men. _____

8. *Detention* is the best form of correction for minor offenses. _____

9. The *vitality* of a nation always depends upon its economic progress. _____

10. Because of their lack of courage, Hitler easily *subjugated* many nations during World War II. _____

EXERCISE B

USING THE CONTEXT

Directions: In the space provided explain the meaning of the italicized word as used in the context of the sentence. Refer to the root meanings.

1. The basic *tenets* of any person's life must be the motivating force of his actions.
   tenet—

2. When citizens are kept in the dark about foreign policy decisions, a *credibility* gap often develops.
   credibility—

3. Notre Dame's *tenacious* goal line stand enabled it to gain a well-deserved victory.
   tenacious—

4. At this *juncture* in our nation's history, we are faced with many crucial decisions.
   juncture—

5. Since he had such excellent *credentials,* the opportunity for the position was enhanced.
   credentials—

6. The colors were so *vivid* that one could almost sense the fall weather.
   vivid—

7. Absolute *fidelity* to one's ideals is one of the marks of a person's greatness.
   fidelity—

8. The demands of the union leaders appeared *inexorable* to the company representatives.
   inexorable—

9. Despite obvious medical and scientific benefits, many people oppose *vivisection* of animals.
   vivisection—

10. Since the case was so important, the lawyer demanded a large *retainer*.
    retainer—

LESSON 19

THE COMING
OF CAESAR

THE FIRST LATIN
AND THE CELTIC INFLUENCE
ON ENGLISH

Soon after the formation of the First Triumvirate (Pompey, Crassus and Caesar) in 60 B.C., the latter went into Gaul to win his military laurels. By the year 54 B.C. he had conquered the whole area from the Mediterranean Sea in Gaul to the Rhine River and the North Sea. Under the pretext of punishing the Britons for helping their Celtic cousins in northern Gaul he conquered Britain. Actually he was more concerned with promoting the glories of Caesar.

Although a Roman foothold on the island was not firmly established until a hundred years later, the language of Rome did have an immediate and lasting influence on these people. The feeling at Rome was that either a person spoke Latin and/or Greek or he was barbarian; therefore, it behooved a man if he wanted to hold a government position or to have any mercantile business with the Roman soldiers to know the language of the conquerors. Just how much Latin influenced the Celts from the time of Caesar to that of King Arthur (c. 500 A.D.) is very difficult to ascertain for no Celtic-written literature of the period exists. The only substantial trace that we have of either Latin or Celtic of this epoch is found in place names like Lancaster (L. castra—camp of Lans), Portsmouth (L. port—carry in place), street (L. strats—strewn of gravel), Bryn Mawr (C.—hill big), Perth (C.—place of hedges), and bat (C.—meaning to fight) in words like *combat* and *debate*.

Although the Celtic people were to be driven from their homelands into the hills of Scotland (Scottish) and Wales (Welsh), they did leave their personality on the land.

111

Expressive Words

Latin Root	Meaning	Examples
alter, altr	other, change	altercation, altruist, alternative
claus, clus, clud	close	claustrophobia, recluse, precluded, secluded
ego	I, self	egocentric, egomaniac, egotistical
flu, fluct	flow	affluent, fluent, fluctuated
jac, ject	throw	interject, rejected, rejection, subject
rupt	break	corruption, disruptive, interrupt, rupture
vers, vert	turn	extrovert, introvert, reverse, transversal

EXERCISE A

PEOPLE IN ACTION

Directions: Test your knowledge of the roots and root meanings by supplying the correct form. Check the list of "Examples"; they contain the answers.

Example:

He was more than just a trusted friend; I considered him my counterpart, my *alter ego* (literally, "other self").

1. Since he was always more interested in helping other people, everyone considered him an _____.

2. Areas of serious disagreement _____ an early end to the strike.

3. Many historians feel that moral _____ caused the downfall of Roman society.

4. President Kennedy was always able to sway an audience because he was considered a _____ speaker.

5. The judge _____ the lawyer's plea after some evidence was declared inadmissible.

6. With no other possible solution in sight the company had no _____ but to close.

7. The theory of the Divine Right of Kings meant that the king was _____ to no higher power than God.

8. After the disastrous defeat on election day, the mayor secluded himself from the news media and _____ himself in a downtown hotel.

9. If "ego" means _____ , "centric" obviously relates to the _____ of things.

10. Some leaders insist that we must _____ the trend toward government subsidies if Americans are to remain strong and independent.

EXERCISE B

MORE OF THE SAME

Directions: For each italicized word first give a meaning based on the root and the context of the sentence, then use your dictionary to list the origin of the word. Change your meanings if necessary.

Example:
She refused to ride in an elevator for she claimed she was a victim of *claustrophobia* as well as acrophobia.
(a) fear of being closed in
(b) L., *claustrum,* "bar or bolt," and N.L. *phobia,* "fear"—more at cloister.

1. Tempers flared as the opposing groups were involved in a serious *altercation* which threatened to erupt into a riot.
   (a)

   (b)

2. Police had to break into the dismal home where the *recluse* had secluded himself for years.
   (a)

   (b)

3. Being *egotistical* he became very peeved and upset when others opposed his wishes.
   (a)

   (b)

4. With a gross national product of many billions America is considered to be an *affluent* society.
   (a)

   (b)

5. *Rejection* of all peace attempts has caused great distress in the world.

    (a)

    (b)

6. With many problems demanding a solution, major world powers cannot risk a *rupture* in international relations.

    (a)

    (b)

7. In geometry a straight line intersecting a system of lines is referred to as a *transversal.*

    (a)

    (b)

8. Because of world conditions the stock market has *fluctuated* considerably in the past year.

    (a)

    (b)

9. The telebinocular has a special shutter which enables the optometrist to *occlude* one eye while examining the other.

    (a)

    (b)

10. As an *extrovert* the president of the Student Government Association felt the need to concern himself with other students' problems.

    (a)

    (b)

LESSON 20

MAKING THEMSELVES AT HOME

THE ANGLO-SAXON INFLUENCE

With the increasing menace of the Germanic tribes in the early part of the fifth century, the Roman legions in Britain and the other extremities of the Empire were withdrawn to defend their homeland. Thus the Celts, already supressed for nearly five hundred years and now having to learn how to fight their own battles became an easy prey to the attacks of the Angles and Saxons. These Teutonic people who, for their own survival, were seeking more suitable farmlands than those they possessed on the swampy and frequently flooded Danish coastline, devised an ingenious plan of conquest later followed by their own American descendents. They banded together and took land only as they needed it, never really allowing the conquered to assess the overall intent of the invaders nor to unite. Those displaced merely moved farther west or north. Like the American Indians, when the Celts finally determined to resist, they discovered they had lost their war.

But not only did the Angles and the Saxons drive the Celts from the land, they also, and then only on very rare occasions, had very little to do with the original inhabitants. They refused to learn the language; if a few Celts wanted to remain on as servants, they had to learn to speak as their masters did. Thus we find, beginning about 450 A.D. with the first Teutonic invasions, a new language being spoken in Britain, or as she was now to be called, Angland. Later, through a monk's copying error, "Angland" became "England."

Since the Angles and the Saxons were basically farmers, it should not be surprising to discover that a vast majority of the words we have inherited from them are short, precise, uncomplicated, common, and almost completely traceable to that "mythical" Indo-European. Almost half the words in a

116

person's speaking vocabulary are Anglo-Saxon in origin; e.g., a, am, did, from, get, is, like, no, of, see, saw, the, there, they. Yet, upwards of seventy-five per cent of the words in a dictionary have been borrowed into English. Probably fifty to sixty per cent of these were Latin in origin with about half of these coming into the language through French. Another considerable percentage of these borrowed words (twenty-five per cent) has come either directly or indirectly through Greek. Old Norse contributed about ten per cent and the remaining words have been culled from many languages all over the world.

Do the following exercises which deal with Latin roots that may help you get to where you are going.

Quo Vadis?

Root	Meaning	Examples
cede, ceed, cess	go	antecedent, proceed, recession
duce, duct	lead	seduce, productive
grad, gress	step	graduate, regression
mis, mit	send	missionary, permit
port	carry	portage, transport
vad, vas	go	pervade, invasion
ven, vent	come	convene, invention

EXERCISE A

A MATCH GAME

From your knowledge of the preceding roots and the prefixes already learned, you should be able to match the words in column A with their meanings, given in column B.

1. aggression   _____
   A. a slight economic depression

2. convention   _____
   B. a ceremonial parade

3. deduction   _____
   C. a violation of a civil law

4. evasion   _____
   D. an unprovoked encroachment on another nation

5. induction   _____
   E. an attempt to avoid duty

6. pervasion   _____
   F. the process of obtaining an endowment from a foundation

7. procession   _____
   G. the act of thoroughly penetrating something

8. recession   _____
   H. the summoning of a group to meet for some common purpose

9. subvention   _____
   I. the process of initiating someone into the armed forces

10. transgression   _____
    J. the deriving of a conclusion from stated premises

EXERCISE B

THE IMPENDING BATTLE

In the following paragraph underline and list the words derived from the roots on the preceding page, and give a meaning for each.

The Impending Battle

At first when I heard the old soldiers telling their war yarns to the new recruits, I thought that they must possess weird imaginations to invent such tales. Therefore, as we readied our heavier weapons to be transported by helicopter for the invasion, I endeavored to dispel some of the new men's fears about the attack. I instructed them to proceed with caution, and gradually. Our mission was a dangerous one, but it was necessary if we were to contain the enemies' aggressive attacks and reduce their forays on our own encampment. The captain's orders were transmitted to each platoon leader that he make frequent contact *via* the walkie-talkie so that no group would ever be more than five minutes distance from relief if a surprise attack should ensue. A recruit's introduction to war was difficult enough without adding to his problems.

1.

2.

3.

4.

5.

6.

7.

8.

9.

10.

LESSON 21
TURNING
ANGLES INTO
ANGELS

SECOND LATIN INFLUENCE

Although the Celts had been Christianized at least a hundred years prior to the Anglo-Saxon invasion, they refused to attempt to convert their sworn enemies. If they could not "beat them," they were determined not to allow the foe to have a share in their eternal bliss in heaven! And so in 597 A.D., under the direction of Pope Gregory I, Augustine of Canterbury was sent from Rome to "change the Angles into Angels."[1] Not only was his coming the advent of Christianity among these people, but it also marked their introduction into the study of literature, history, and philosophy. Since the language of the church and its monastery schools was Latin, both it and the religious teaching of the church began and, for a millenium, continued to have an imposing influence on the development of the native language.

Excepting the anonymous *Beowulf* composer, the two great poets of the Anglo-Saxon Period (450-1066 A.D.) Caedmon and Cynwulf are primarily noted for their religious hymns and biblical homilies. The greatest scholar and first historian of the kingdom, Venerable Bede, (673-735 A.D.,) wrote over forty books, all but one in Latin. And the most important philosophical contribution was King Alfred's (848-901 A.D.) translation of Boethius' *Consolation of Philosophy*. Although Boethius' work was basically pagan in scope, Alfred wisely—or so he believed—contributed various religious interpretations for his readers' edification. While the most important prose work of the era, the *Anglo-Saxon Chronicle*, (c. 825-1150 A.D.) was written in the vernacular, it clearly demonstrates the monastic backgrounds of its clerical authors and

[1] Laird, Charlton, *The Miracle of Language* (Fawcett World Library: New York, 1957), p. 43.

120

exemplifies the gradual changes in spelling, grammar, and syntax from Old English into Middle English.

Thus, we find that during the course of the Anglo-Saxon period the Teutonic language was continually being refined and augmented by the bilingual writers, most of whom were clerics. Indeed, our word *clerical,* meaning "white collared office worker," is itself an indication of church influence on education, for the first schools were religious ones; Oxford was not founded until 1163 and Cambridge in 1209, and even they were initially religious in nature and orientation.

Before continuing our discussion on the various influences on the English language, do the following exercise which introduces Latin roots which may be connected with some mathematical terminologies.

A Little Math

Latin Root	Meaning	Examples
curr, curs	run, happen	current, precursor, recurrence
equ	equal	equanimity, equation, equilibrium
fer, lat	carry, bear	transfer, translation, circumference
frac, frag	break	fragile, fragmented, refractory, fraction
pon, pos	place, put	composite, deposit, proponent, exponent
seg, sect	cut	dissect, segment, vivisection, bisect
tang, tact, ting	touch, feel	tangible, contingency, tangent
tol	endure	tolerate, extol

EXERCISE A

BE SELECTIVE

Directions: Complete the following sentences, using the proper words from the "Examples" column. Contextual aids are also provided.

1. It is essential to maintain _____ if the space capsule is to dock with the mother ship.

2. Because of constant failure, the President brought about an immediate

    _____ of duties.

3. Patrick Henry was a _____ of the principles of the American Revolution.

4. The police artist put together a _____ sketch of the criminal.

5. Despite her _____ appearance, she was capable of intensive work.

6. A successful military leader must always be prepared for every

    _____ in battle.

7. There is one _____ of the population that will always be dissatisfied with any approach.

8. No amount of persuasion could make him _____ the new order of things in the country.

9. Anne Morrow Lindbergh believes that a woman leads a _____

    _____ existence because of the many and often minor duties she has to perform.

10. The _____ unrest in our society could lead to greater strife or a better life for all.

122

EXERCISE B

RIGHT OR WRONG?

With your knowledge of the above roots, answer the following either *True* or *False*. Key words, drawn from the roots, are italicized.

1. All *extracurricular* activities must be done in school. _____
2. A *cursory* reading of a lesson is one given to much detail. _____
3. *Concurrent* assignments have some details in common. _____
4. When the sum of the quantities of two members of a mathematical problem are *equal* we have an *equation.* _____
5. During the vernal *equinox* the duration of day and night are approximately the same. _____
6. A person who loses his *equilibrium* is likely to fall. _____
7. A *vociferous* person is usually an introvert. _____
8. An improper *fraction occurs* when the denominator exceeds the numerator. _____
9. Since many of the ancient Greek dramas survive only in *fragmentary* documents we may some day possess a rendition of them. _____
10. A *fractious* person usually does not have many friends. _____
11. The diameter of a circle is any *bisectional* line, which divides it into two equal parts. _____
12. A twelve inch ruler may be *segmented* into twelve equal parts by eleven cuts. _____
13. A *sector* of a circle includes at least two radii and the arc of the circle. _____
14. A line that is *tangent* to a circle is parallel to its circumference. _____
15. Optical is to the sense of sight as *tactile* is to the sense of touch. _____

123

LESSON 22

THE VIKINGS–
PIRATES OF
THE NORTH

THE NORSE INFLUENCE

One morning in the year 787 A.D., the lords of the Anglo-Saxon kingdoms awoke to discover that the renowned and very rich Abbey of Lindisforne in Northumberland had been plundered by their distant relatives, the Norseman from Scandinavia. Before the Angles and the Saxons could mobilize, the Vikings, as they were called, had disappeared into the sea. For the next century England as well as vast areas of continental Europe (France, Germany, Spain, Italy, and Russia) were plagued by the unorthodox military tactics of these people.

With a few shallow bottom boats, loaded with warriors, the Vikings, usually under the protection of night and on the crest of a high tide, would row into a harbor or up a river and pillage the unsuspecting and frequently poorly protected coastal towns, villages, and monasteries. By the following morning, before a token force of resistance could be organized, they had sailed away. They were finally checked (they were never really subdued) by the ingenuity of Alfred the Great (King from 871-899 A.D.), who outsmarted them in geopolitics. First he christianized them so that they could be threatened with damnation if they did not cease their lives of evil, and then he conceded "good farm lands" in the mid-highland district to them—the last outpost of the Celts which did not belong to the Anglo-Saxons anyway.[1]

Since the Vikings were basically simple-minded people, many of the Old Norse traces which are found in English are common and ordinary words. For example, their word for town was *ham,* which we still have in such place names as Nottingham, Birmingham, Durham, etc. The most notable adoption is the use

[1] Briton, Crane, *et al., A History of Civilization* (Prentice-Hall, Inc.: Englewood Cliffs, New Jersey, 1967), p. 190-192.

of their plural third person pronouns, *they, their,* and *them* for the Anglo-Saxon equivalents *hie, hiera,* and *heom* which were frequently confused with the singular forms *he* (hem), *heo* (heom), and *hit.* Since both the language of the Vikings and that of the Angles and Saxons sprang from an earlier Germanic tongue, it is difficult to ascertain whether such common words as coast, storm, flood, ebb, cat, hound, apple, fruit, boat, deck come to us through the Anglo-Saxons or through their cousins, the Norsemen.

Do the following vocabulary exercises which contain Latin roots that will enable you to suffer in style.

Ways to Suffer

Latin Roots	Meaning	Examples
cap, capt, cept, cip	take	incapacitate, captivate, imperceptive, emancipation
cide, cis	kill, cut	homicide, incision, suicidal
leg	law	legal, legislature, illegitimate
mort, mor	death	mortal, mortician, moribund
pend, pens, pond	hang, weigh	appendix, pensive, imponderable
tors, tort	twist	torsion, tortuous, contorsion
tract	drag	extract, protractor

EXERCISE A

PICK YOUR VICTIM

Can you identify each of the following victims?

1. fratricide

2. germicide

3. infanticide

4. insecticide

5. matricide

6. patricide

7. pesticide

8. regicide

9. suicide

10. virucide

HOW DID THEY FEEL?

Define the italicized words. Be on the look out for contextual clues. You may use your dictionary. Caution: English meanings may have greater extension than that found in their original root meanings.

Example:

Little has been mentioned as to why the Black Revolution is only beginning now, a hundred years after the *Emancipation Act.*

Emancipation—freedom from bondage, literally to take from a hand.

1. The young lady was completely *mortified* by the severity of the professor's remark.
   mortified—

2. For his continual verbal *retorts* the judge leveled an additional five dollar fine.
   retorts—

3. Because of the *deception* in the article he was himself severely criticized by the press.
   deception—

4. The malignancy had to be delicately *excised* from the surrounding non-infected tissues.
   excised—

5. The *legality* of euthanasia has frequently been questioned but never has it won federal or state approval.
   legality—

6. The victim writhed in agony and fell to the floor in a *contortive* fit.
   contortive—

7. Since both her legs had been broken, it was necessary to place them in *traction.*
   traction—

8. Since he had been injured while lifting heavy boxes at work, he was entitled to workmen's *compensation.*
compensation—

9. Because he was just recovering from a bad cold, he was very *susceptible* to the pulmonary virus.
susceptible—

10. "It was the painted figure of Time, as he is commonly represented, save that, in lieu of the scythe, he held what, at a casual glance, I supposed to be the pictured image of a huge *pendulum,* such as we see on an antique clock."
(Pit and the Pendulum.)
pendulum—

LESSON 23

ENGLAND
BECOMES
SOPHISTICATED

THE FRENCH INFLUENCE

No sooner had the Anglo-Saxons learned to live in harmony with their Viking cousins then they were confronted with another and a more serious nemesis, one which would eventually change the very structure of the island kingdom. Some Norsemen, who had been ravaging the coasts of England, claimed a portion of northern France, still known as Normandy, for their homeland. In this way the Norman-French language, culture, tradition, military, and political power became entwined with the English heritage.

Upon the death, in 1066 A.D., of Edward, a Saxon, who had no heir, the English throne was up for grabs. Harold, an Angle, proclaimed himself king, but his accession was challenged by William the Duke of Normandy on two grounds: first, he maintained that Edward had promised him the succession; secondly, he claimed that through heritage he was related to the Dane, Canute, who had preceded Edward. To enforce his claim, William, with his knights in armor, met, on October 14, Harold's, outmanned, outmaneuvered, and ill-armed soldiers in the Valley of Hastings. Before the day was over Harold had been slain, his army defeated, and England had a new king.[1]

Although the conquest was one of the great turning points in English history, it had no more than a political effect on the common people, much like a transition in our own country of a Democratic president to a Republican or vice versa.

Anyone who did not directly oppose the new regime was permitted to go about his business as he pleased. There was but one catch. The new lords,

---

[1] Savelle, Max, (gen. ed.), *A History of World Civilization*, (Holt, Rinehart & Winston: N.Y., 1963), Vol. 1, p. 456-457.

the administrators of the government, the continental merchants, the preachers, and the teachers mainly spoke French and frequently required those who wished to deal with them to speak French. Thus, we find the people becoming bilingual and even trilingual. They spoke one language at home, another at work, and the third in church and in school.

For almost three hundred years French was and could very well have continued to be the language of England had it not been for the Hundred Years' War (1337-1453). The occasion for the outbreak of hostilities was Edward III's claim to the throne of France, through his mother, the daughter of Philip IV. But the majority of the French lords ruled that tradition excluded women from the lineage of succession and, therefore, the crown was presented to Philip's brother. War quickly ensued.

As the war dragged on, everything French, including the language, began to be looked at in disdain. Why should a lord's son be educated at Paris, the seat of the adversary? And so Oxford and Cambridge began to gain status, especially since the former could claim Roger Bacon and Duns Scotus, two of the greatest scholars of the entire medieval era, as alumni.

By the turn of the fifteenth century we find that, although French was considered alien, it had left a tremendous deposit of ecclesiastical, governmental, legal, literary, and scientific words in the English language. Between thirty to forty percent of the words in the dictionary are traceable to French or to French from Latin derivations. Finally, the Normans also helped to bring culture to England. They introduced the mystery and the morality plays, the debate, fables, and satire, which enabled Englishmen to express their thoughts with a greater refinement of language.

Do the following exercises based on some more common Latin roots. Nearly forty per cent of the examples have come to us from the French.

Where the Action Is

Latin Root	Meaning	Examples
ag, act	act, drive	agitation, agent, transaction
hab, hib	have, hold	habitual, exhibition, inhabit
her, hes	cling, stick	adhere, adhesive, cohesion
leg, lect, lig	choose, read	elegance, lectern, eligible
mon, monit	warn	monster, summon, admonition
pel, puls	drive	impel, appellate, compulsory

130

Latin Root	Meaning	Examples
pet, pit	seek	petition, repetitious, propitious
quir, ques, quis	search out, question	require, inquest, inquisition
sequ, secut, sue	follow	obsequious, persecute, ensue
sta, stat, sist	stand	instability, statute, persistence
vinc, vict	conquer	vincible, victim, eviction

131

EXERCISE A

TAKE YOUR PICK

Underline the proper word which best completes each sentence.

1. A special section of the new wing was set aside for (prohibition, rehabilitation) cases so that they could more readily acclimate themselves to society.
2. She complained and was (petulant, competent) and she pushed him away ... (Buck, *Good Earth*).
3. Before you elect to take Advanced Calculus II, you must satisfy the (requisites, prerequisites).
4. As Americans we hold that the rights of life, liberty and the pursuit of happiness are (adherent, inherent) characteristics.
5. If you wish to become a better student, you must first (desist, subsist) from your poor reading habits.
6. An (appellant, petitioner) is a person who feels that a lower court of law has adversely ruled against him and so seeks to have a higher court reverse that decision.
7. A political faction which tends to suggest drastic changes in foreign policies, and which advocates a completely new approach is usually labeled (stable, reactionary).
8. The (ensuing, pursuing) aftereffects of the earthquake were more devastating than the initial tremor.
9. Since he had not resided in the state for more than one year he was declared (eligible, ineligible).
10. His sudden unprovoked outburst of anger resulted in an (admonition, premonition) from the presiding judge.

EXERCISE B

YOU MAKE UP THE WORD

In many of the preceding exercises some unfamiliar words were given and you were either to give a meaning for them, or to determine the validity of a statement in which they were used. This time the literal meaning of a word is given; e.g., "to *stand against,* in the way of something, n.," and you are to write down the word, *obstacle.* For your convenience, key words are italicized and the part of the speech required is noted (n.–noun). After checking the above root list, you may use your dictionary.

Literal Meaning	Part of Speech	Word
1. *unable* to be *conquered*	adj.	
2. the act of *driving* something *forward*	n.	
3. a person, who *together* with others, *seeks* to win an event	n.	
4. a *forewarning* of something	n.	
5. *holding* or doing something constantly	adv.	
6. to take a *stand on* an issue	v.	
7. *seeking information*	n.	
8. succeeding, *following* directly *(below)* another event	adj.	
9. having the quality of *clinging* firmly *together*	n.	
10. the body of men *chosen* by the people to *vote in* the president	n.	

133

LESSON 24

FROM CHAUCER TO SHAKESPEARE TO . . . YOU

ENGLISH—
A LIVING LANGUAGE

From its origin the English language has developed and has changed rapidly. Few people today, or, for that matter, hardly any Englishmen in the last thousand years have been able to pick up a copy of *Beowulf* and read it without first learning the language, yet the Frisians of Holland can do so. Chaucer, the so-called father of Modern English, is probably best studied in transliteration; Shakespeare frequently has to be "updated" to be appreciated by theater goers; and Defoe's *Moll Flanders* and Fielding's award winning *Tom Jones* were modernized for their movie audiences. English has been and continues to be a language in a state of flux; and therefore, when we attempt to broaden our knowledge of it we must be aware of its viable nature.

Study of roots and affixes should enhance our vocabulary, but we must be careful. Should we not be more concerned with the meaning of a word like *routine* than in the knowledge that it probably traces its origin to the Latin, *ruptus* meaning "break," from which our ancestors, also, probably decided that a "broken way" was a well "trodden way" and therefore "common"? Moreover, a word's usage may have changed during the course of centuries, as has happened to *enviable* (from the Latin *in* and *videre,* to see in). Do not confuse roots. *Inherent* and *inherit* do not both come from the Latin "her" meaning "cling." *Relieve* and *believe* are not related, nor is ventilation linked with the root "vent" meaning to "come," but rather with *ventulus - little wind.* Knowledge of roots can be advantageous when used cautiously, wisely, and usually also in conjunction with contextual clues. Learning words in isolation is frequently a meaningless task, for words usually only have meaning when used with others.

Mindful of the above, do the last two exercises concerned with Latin roots.

Last But Not Least

Latin Root	Meaning	Examples
cad, cas, cid	fall	cadance, casualty, occidental
cert	certain, decide	ascertain, certify, incertitude
cresc, cre, cret	grow	crescent, increment, accretion
doc, doct	teach, prove	documentary, doctrine, postdoctoral
mov, mot, (mob)	move	remove, promote, mobilize
stru, struct	build	misconstrue, instrument, obstructive
temp, tempor, (temper)	time	tempestuous, temporal, distemper
tend, tens, tent	stretch	extend, tension, intent
us, ut	use	abusive, usury, utilitarian
vid, vis, (vi)	see	evident, advisory, purview

EXERCISE A

HOW'S THAT AGAIN?

Without the aid of your dictionary try to determine the meaning of the following italicized words. You may refer to the above roots for guidance. Contextual clues are frequently provided.

1. ... the mighty Yosemite River *cascading* into the depths.
   cascading–

2. ... accomplished only through *concerted* effort.
   concerted–

3. ... swelling to a final *crescendo* of sound.
   crescendo–

4. ... *indoctrinated* in all facets of communism.
   indoctrinated–

5. ... decorated with multicolored and multishaped *mobiles.*
   mobiles–

6. A *contemporary* critic of Hemingway ...
   contemporary–

7. Dirt can't hide from *intensified* Tide!
   intensified–

8. ... being *instrumental* in bringing the two sides together.
   instrumental–

9. In the tales of Robin Hood, Sir John tries to *usurp* King Richard's throne.
   usurp–

10. Unfortunately, the *provisions* of his will did not please the relatives.
    provisions–

EXERCISE B

THE CHANGING TIMES

With the aid of your dictionary indicate how the following words have arrived at the listed meaning.

1. decadent—deteriorating—

2. discern—discriminate—

3. concrescence—coalescence, fusion—

4. docile—obedient—

5. promotion—advancement—

6. extemporaneous—impromptu—

7. tendency—a particular outlook—

8. construe—analyze a sentence—

9. perusal—a careful studying—

10. enviable—highly desirable—

UNIT V

THE GREEK CONTRIBUTION

LESSON 25

GREEK
PREFIXES
AND ROOTS

USE YOUR HEAD!

Greek, as well as Latin, has had great effect on the development of the English and the Romance languages. Since for almost four centuries, *circa* 100 B.C. to *circa* 300 A.D., Greek was the language of the nobility of Rome, it is not surprising that many of our words have come to us from the Greek *via* Latin. For example

English	*Latin*	*Greek*
critic	criticus (judge)	krites (judge)
dogma	dogmata (tenet)	dokein (to seem)
gymnasium	gymnasium (exercise ground)	gumnos (naked)
iridescent	iris (rainbow)	Iris (the messenger goddess)
kleptomaniac	clepere (take and mariacus)	kleptes (thief) and mania (frenzy)
mystic	mysticus (secret)	musterion (keeping silence)
scholar	schola (school)	schole (leisure)
theatrical	theatrum (theatre)	theatron (view)

Since many of the sciences had their origins or their major developments in Ancient Greece, many of their nomenclatures were derived from that language. With the exception of algebra and calculus, the other branches of mathematics are all Greek: arithmetic, geometry, trigonometry, dynamics, ballistics, physics, thermodynamics, optics, geodesy, geophysics, astronomy, etc. The scientists of the sixteenth, seventeenth, and eighteenth centuries who frequently were in open conflict with the Roman church, turned to the Greek roots for their new terminologies. This trend has continued; in fact, it has snowballed into the atomic age with one slight difference. Whereas Copernicus, Newton, and their

139

followers actually read Aristotle, Euclid, and Plato, many of our so-called modern scientists merely refer to a Greek lexicon to make up the "unpronounceable" name for their new facial cream, mouthwash, pep pills, or what-have-you. Most of us really do not care what it is that washes our whites whiter or makes our hair less greasy.

Many words of Greek origin can be recognized and their meanings clarified by their prefixes. Addendum 4, "Common Greek Prefixes," contains a listing of those that are especially important. Refer to this Addendum. Before doing either of the exercises, look up in your dictionary any word which remains unfamiliar to you, for many of the words appearing in the "Examples" column are used in the two exercises.

EXERCISE A

THE COMMON GREEK PREFIXES
TRUE OR FALSE?

By referring to the list of "The Common Greek Prefixes" located in Addendum 4, and noting the context, you should be able to decide whether or not the following sentences are correct. Place a "T" for *True* after each correct statement and an "F" for *False* after the incorrect one. Key words using Greek prefixes are italicized.

1. Since an *agnostic* believes that the knowledge of God is un-attainable, he is considered an atheist. _____
2. Although we may not think of him as such today, George Washington could well have been labeled an *anarchist* for leading the Americans against the British monarch. _____
3. One of the major aspects of most best selling murder mysteries is their *anticlimactic* endings. _____
4. An *apostate* is one who freely becomes a missionary for his religion in some foreign land. _____
5. A college student is responsible for satisfying all the degree requirements which are stipulated in his freshman *catalog*. _____
6. Probably the most famous *cataracts* (arassein–Gr.) in the United States and Canada are Niagara Falls. _____
7. In order for the line within a circle to be labeled a *diameter* it must pass through the center of that circle. _____
8. A *diagnostic* reading test merely surveys one's reading ability. _____
9. A papal *encyclical* is intended more for the entire Catholic communities of the world than for just the Catholics of Rome. _____
10. An *epilogue* would usually precede the actual text of a book. _____
11. It is considered proper to attempt to *eulogize* a man's life during his funeral oration. _____
12. If heterogeneous grouping in school is the mixing of students with various backgrounds, skills, and abilities, then *homogeneous* grouping should attempt to place youngsters with somewhat similar backgrounds, skills, and abilities in the same class. _____

141

13. A person who is known for speaking in *hyperboles* is likely to be praised for his credulity. _____

14. *Hypocrisy* is a virtue found acceptable to all religious faiths. _____

15. The urban area stretching from Portland, Maine to Norfolk, Virginia along the Atlantic sea coast can be correctly referred to as a *megapolis*. _____

16. "A ship plowing the sea" may be called a *metaphor* for literal change of the word "plowing" has occurred. _____

17. *Microbiology* would probably be a branch of biology which deals especially with forms of life which are not easily discernible to the naked eye. _____

18. If the Greek word "lithikos" means "stone," then we could properly refer to our age of civilization as *Neolithic*. _____

19. A student who evidences deficiencies in spelling would probably benefit from a course in *orthography*. _____

20. A reading course is always a *panacea* for students who are having difficulty in college. ("akos" means "remedy") _____

21. Not all baseball players agree with the *paradox*, "Good guys finish last." _____

22. A *perimeter* is to a square as a circumference is to a circle. _____

23. A *polyclinic* is a hospital which treats only patients with terminal cancer. _____

24. If you *sympathize* with a person involved in an accident, you condone his reckless driving. _____

25. A *telescope* is to a star as a *periscope* is to the sea. _____

EXERCISE B

WHAT'S IN A WORD?

Directions: After listing the (a) prefixes and (b) roots, (c) give a modern meaning based on context for each of the italicized words. Refer to your dictionary whenever necessary. The root may not be from the Greek.

Example:

The *neoclassical* author attempted to express himself according to the ancient standards of Greek and Roman literature and culture.

(a) Prefix—neo—new
(b) Root—classicus (L.)
(c) A revival of classical style in literature, art, etc.

1. It is readily acknowledged that *hypertension* may be caused by the fast pace of modern living.
   (a) Prefix
   (b) Root
   (c)

2. Yet, a truly involved person can not stay on the *periphery* of modern society if he is to make an intelligent contribution.
   (a) Prefix
   (b) Root
   (c)

3. *Megalomania* is a characteristic of men like Hitler and Mussolini who sought world domination.
   (a) Prefix
   (b) Root
   (c)

4. More than words, the visit to the prison was a graphic *analysis* of one of America's great social and moral ills.
   (a) Prefix
   (b) Root
   (c)

5. His *antagonistic* attitude was more of a bluff since he was essentially an insecure person.

   (a) Prefix
   (b) Root
   (c)

6. After the Jewish people returned from captivity, the Great *Synagogue* of one hundred twenty members was presided over by Ezra.

   (a) Prefix
   (b) Root
   (c)

7. The Church of St. Mark's itself is an *epitome* of the changes of Venetian architecture. (Ruskin)

   (a) Prefix
   (b) Root
   (c)

8. An *orthodontist* is a highly regarded member of the dental profession.

   (a) Prefix
   (b) Root
   (c)

9. Lengthy *diatribes* are often used by dictators to arouse the people to an emotional pitch.

   (a) Prefix
   (b) Root
   (c)

10. The diabetic found it necessary to carry a card, signed by his doctor, explaining his reasons for possessing a *hypodermic* needle.

    (a) Prefix
    (b) Root
    (c)

LESSON 26

LEARNING TO COUNT AGAIN

THE COMMON GREEK NUMERALS

Although the Greek numerals are not used as frequently as their Latin counterparts, being able to recognize them, especially when they are used as prefixes, may enable you to arrive at the meaning of many scientific and literary words.

Greek Prefix	Meaning	Examples
hemi	half	hemicycle, hemisphere
mono	one	monocle, monologues
di	two	digraph, dichotomy
tri (same in L.)	three	trilogy, trigonometry
tetra	four	tetragonal, tetraoxide
penta	five	pentateuch, pentameter
hexa	six	hexahedron, hexameter
hepta	seven	heptarchy, heptad
octa, octo (same in L.)	eight	octagon, octave
ennea	nine	ennead
deca, deka	ten	decalogue, decade
hecto, heka	hundred	hectograph, hecatomb

EXERCISE A

TAKE A COUNT

By selecting the proper word from the "Examples" column, complete the following sentences.

1. *Oedipus the King* is only one third of Sophocles' great _____ _____ on this mythical tragic hero.

2. As a comedian Bob Hope is unsurpassed for his humorous _____ _____ at the beginning of his shows.

3. A book divided into nine chapters could be labeled an _____ _____ .

4. In the previous presidential election a serious _____ of interests had split the business community.

5. Shakespeare was the master of the blank verse, an unrhymed iambic _____ verse consisting of five measured feet.

6. In the International Science Vocabulary a compound of an element with four atoms of oxygen is called a _____ .

7. The loosely-knit confederation of the seven Anglo-Saxon kingdoms in the seventh and eighth centuries is referred to in history as an _____ _____ .

8. The Decalogue, which God entrusted to Moses for mankind, are more commonly known as the _____ .

9. Insects are correctly classified as _____ since they have three pairs of feet.

10. The Americas, both North, Central, and South, were classified as the western _____ by fifteenth and sixteenth century European geographers.

EXERCISE B

HOW MANY?

Without looking back to the list of Greek numerals, place the correct number, or the words which will complete each sentence.

1. The Heptateuch are the first _____ books of the Bible from Genesis to Judges.

2. The U.S. military chiefs-of-staff have their headquarters in the *Pentagon,* a large _____ sided building outside Washington, D.C.

3. A person suffering from hemiplegia is paralyzed _____ of his body.

4. Most religious groups are alike insofar as they are monotheistic in their beliefs in _____ God.

5. An octandrious flower should have _____ stamens.

6. In Greek mythology the sea-god, Poseidon, is portrayed as carrying a trident, _____ pitchfork, which he supposedly used to goad on his servants.

7. The most outstanding athlete of the Olympics is usually the man who wins the decathlon, an athletic contest consisting of _____ different events.

8. If a decagram has the American equivalency of .353 ounces, then a hectogram would weigh _____ ounces.

9. . . . and Herod, tetrarch of Galilee, and Philip, his brother, tetrarch of the districts of Iturea and Trachonitis, and Lysonias tetrarch of Abilene . . . (Luke, 3) indicates that at the birth of Christ that part of the Roman Empire was subdivided into _____ sections.

10. A pentacle and a hexagram may both have the form of a star. The difference between these two figures is that the latter has _____ more point.

LESSON 27

BE SPECIFIC!

COMMON GREEK ROOTS PART 1

People, *even students,* do not like to "get the run around." If you wanted a copy of your college transcript forwarded to another school, you would not expect the registrar to send you first to your instructors, then to your adviser, and finally to the dean of students. No, you would expect him to have your grades on file and to be able to comply with your request within a reasonable time. Although we, as Americans, expect things to be done now and in the correct way, we are often guilty of "beating around the bush" in our own writing and speaking. If we have something to say we should say it, otherwise we're just wasting someone's precious time. Students are sometimes justly accused of padding a term paper or composition, often confusing the issue rather than clarifying. A classic example of this is often seen in government directives.

An aide of President Franklin Roosevelt drafted a wartime communique that read (if you can call it reading): "Such preparations shall be made as will completely obscure all Federal buildings and non-Federal buildings occupied by the Federal Government during an air raid for any period of time from visibility by reason of internal or external illumination. Such obscuration may be obtained either by blackout construction or by termination of the illumination. This will, of course, require that in building areas in which production must continue during the blackout, construction must be provided that internal illumination may continue. Other areas, whether or not occupied by personnel, may be obscured by terminating the illumination."

Terminating the obscuration, F.D.R. wrote:

"Tell them that in buildings where they have to keep the work going, to put something across the window. In buildings where they can afford to let the work stop for a while, turn out the lights."

"But then, was not the assignment to be 500 words or five pages?" is a frequent rebuttal.

This is not what is meant by being word-conscious! Rather, your words should say what you mean. Be specific!

In the following exercise substitute a more precise word for the underlined phrases. The following list of roots and their general meanings should provide some aids for you. Where possible, contextual clues have been provided.

Greek Roots

Roots	Meaning	Examples
chron	time	chronological, synchronize
gram, graph	write	epigram, telegraph
log	speech, study	monologue, biology
gon	side	pentagon, trigonometry
meter, metr	measure	perimeter, geometry
nom	law, rule	autonomy, astronomer
onym	name	synonym, anonymous
phon, phono	sound	phonics, euphony
scope	see, watch	telescope, microscope

EXERCISE A

THE GREEKS HAD
A WORD FOR IT

Directions: Complete each of the following sentences by selecting the proper word from the "Examples" column. The word's meaning is given in parenthesis.

1. The history professor required his students to be able to unscramble a list of dates, names, and events and to put them in their proper *(sequential arrangement* or *regular)* divisions. (_____)

2. The death-blow to the Pony Express Service has often been attributed to the installation and connection of a *(sending and receiving wireless message)* system from the mid-continent to the Pacific coast.

    (_____)

3. He would never let anyone else *(say a word)* as he proceeded with his boring

    (_____).

4. As a mathematics major he was required to take a course in *(the study of the properties, functions and applications of triangles)*. (_____)

5. The problem asked for the *(measurement of the distance around)*

    and (_____) of the *(five sided figure)*.

6. (_____)

7. Besides being in charge of the planetarium he was also a bona fide *(scientist who studied the laws governing the movements of the stars)*.

    (_____)

8. Rather than learn the rules of orthography, some students develop their own system of *(spelling words by sounding them out)*. (_____)

9. Many living cells which are invisible to the naked eye are readily observed with a *(special optical instrument which magnifies images of minute objects)*.

    (_____)

10. The author of *Beowulf,* the epic of Old English literature, is *(a writer whose name has been lost in history)*. (_____)

EXERCISE B

BREAK THEM DOWN!

Directions: For each of the following words (a) list the origin of each of its main parts then (b) write a well-constructed sentence that shows your complete knowledge of the word. Use your dictionary.

Example:

seismograph

(a) seismos GK earthquake, vibration + graphein Gk to write
(b) The Fordham University *seismographic* equipment recorded violent tremors and shock waves in the vicinity of Alaska, indicating possible extensive damage.

1. *astronomical*

    (a)

    (b)

2. *bibliography*

    (a)

    (b)

3. *chronometer*

    (a)

    (b)

4. *homonym*

    (a)

    (b)

5. *pathological*

    (a)

    (b)

6. *phonograph*

   (a)

   (b)

7. *symmetry*

   (a)

   (b)

8. *symphony*

   (a)

   (b)

9. *telescopic*

   (a)

   (b)

10. *trigonometry*

    (a)

    (b)

SUPPLEMENTARY EXERCISE

Are you familiar with these words or expressions? Write a meaning for each.

1. anachronism

2. apologetics

3. eulogy

4. euphony and cacophony

5. kaleidoscope

6. lithography

7. metric mile

8. phonetic alphabet

9. pseudonym

10. telemetry

LESSON 28

GREEK
TO ME:

COMMON GREEK ROOTS
PART II

For generations, students, when confronted with an extremely difficult paragraph have uttered in dismay, "It's Greek to me!" Fortunately, they may discover that neither the passage, the vocabulary, nor the complaint may be as hopeless as it sounds. Often an application of good reading skills, which involve vocabulary study, may clarify the meaning.

Since authors endeavor to write within a definite frame of reference, never allow yourself to become "bogged down" with a paragraph. Frequently, they will define important words or indicate by type of print that the precise meaning will be found in the glossary. Also, contextual clues within that paragraph or subsequent paragraphs may clarify a word's meaning. These two approaches should be utilized before referring to a dictionary. If after careful analysis it is still obscure, make a notation in your book to ask the instructor for clarification. Then continue careful reading.

But let's come back to this matter of Greek. A little knowledge of some of the basic Greek roots can be a great help in strengthening your vocabulary and thus assist you in studying and reading. Here is a list of a few important roots with their common meanings.

Roots	Meanings	Examples
agogue	leader, lead	pedagogue
auto	self	autobiography
crac, crat	power, rule	aristocrat
dem	people	democracy
dox, dog	belief, truth	paradox, dogma
gen	kind, race	homogeneous
pyr	fire	pyrex
tax, tac	arrange	thermotaxis

154

EXERCISE A

PICK THE KIN

Part I: Look closely at each of the following italicized words. If you think that it is derived from one of the above roots, circle it and write its meaning.

1. in the *automat*

2. *demonology* of Satan

3. religious *doxology*

4. French *gendarme*

5. science of *eugenics*

6. great *pyramids* of Egypt

7. funeral *pyre*

8. stuffed by a *taxidermist*

9. *tactical* maneuvers

10. *taciturn*

Part II: Match the form of government with its proper terminology.

11. a government having a hereditary ruler "for life" with nominal or absolute power _____

12. the government in which the power is vested in only a few _____

A. aristocracy

B. democracy

C. monarchy

13. the government in which the
power is vested in the rich   _____   D. oligarchy

14. the government of an elite,   E. plutocracy
privileged class   _____

15. a government by officials re-   F. theocracy
garded as divinely guided   _____

EXERCISE B

BREAK THEM DOWN!

Directions: Based on contextual clues and your knowledge of prefixes and roots give a general meaning of the italicized words. After completing the exercise, you may check your answers with your dictionary.

1. For his action against the major steel companies, John F. Kennedy was called a *demagogue* in some newspaper editorials.

2. *Syntax* is that part of grammar which deals primarily with the structure of a phrase, clause, or sentence.

3. The jury found the *pyromaniac* guilty of igniting four separate warehouses.

4. The *orthodox* Jews hold their services in a
and
5. *synagogue.*

6. The students began a "sit down" strike against the chancellor of the university for his *autocratic* attitude toward them as well as toward the faculty.

7. The people of the African colonies are rightly agitating for *autonomy* in their own lands.

8. After paying such an enormous sum for the tracing of his family's *genealogy*, he was quite upset to learn that one of his forefathers was executed on the guillotine.

9. Although he shot in a very *unorthodox* style, he was by far the best player on the basketball court.

10. A sociologist concerned with the overpopulation of a country such as India, would do well to consult the current *demography* before making any rash predictions.

SUPPLEMENTARY EXERCISE

Directions: List the origin of these five words and use each one in a well-constructed sentence.

1. genocide

2. autopsy

3. paradoxical

4. technocracy

5. pyrotechnics

6. autonomous

7. dogmatism

8. degenerate

9. pedagogy

10. pyrosis

LESSON 29

IS THERE A DOCTOR IN THE HOUSE?

GREEK ROOTS FOUND IN MEDICAL TERMINOLOGY

A favorite line in many of the tear-jerking movies of yesteryear was, "Is there a doctor in the house?" This was usually uttered as the hero began to succumb while others bravely lived the old slogan, "the show must go on." But what would actually happen if this plea had to be made at anyone of our neighborhood theaters today? Who would answer?

Unfortunately, in many of our urban neighborhoods the good old-fashioned doctor is, or has become, a thing of the past. No longer are members of the medical profession satisfied with just an M.D. No, the trend is toward specialization. The patient has to be somewhat of his own doctor, for not only does he have to feel sick, but he must also know what ails him so that he can make an appointment to visit the proper specialist.

In order to facilitate your choice in time of pain, let us, with the aid of some Greek roots, introduce you to some of these iatrists (healers).

Roots

Greek Root	Meaning	Examples
chiro	hand	chiropractor
derm	skin	dermatologist
don	tooth	orthodontist
neur, neuro	nerve	neurologist

159

Greek Root	Meaning	Examples
optic, opto	eye	optometrist
osteo	bone	osteopath
path	disease, suffering	pathologist
ped	child	pediatrician
pod	foot	podiatrist
psych	soul	psychologist

EXERCISE A

MEDICAL SPECIALIST

By inserting the names of the proper specialists complete the following sentences.

1. A person afflicted with a severe case of poison ivy over his entire body may well be advised to see a _____.

2. A _____ is a physician who attempts to diagnose and treat diseases which seem to be centered in a patient's nervous system.

3. Many a Hollywood actress owes the secret of her charming smile to the dental dexterity of her _____.

4. A person suffering with a dislocated spinal disk might visit a _____ who would endeavor to ease the pain by manipulating the spinal column.

5. An optician grinds lenses to the prescription determined during the course of an examination conducted usually by the _____.

6. Before permanent injury sets in, a person suffering from minor mental and/or emotional disturbances should visit a _____ .

7. Almost every hospital is staffed by a _____ whose prime task is to attempt to diagnose the patient's probable disease and to recommend treatment.

8. Dr. Benjamin Spock, the author of *Baby and Child Care,* is probably the world's most renowned _____.

9. An _____ is a physician who specializes in bone disorders.

10. Corns and callouses of the feet are probably best treated by a skillful _____.

EXERCISE B

WORDS, WORDS, WORDS!

(1) From your knowledge of Greek roots and prefixes, see if you can write a definition for each of the following words. (2) They are not necessarily all medical terms. (3) You may check the answers with your dictionary after attempting all fifteen.

1. apathy

2. chirography

3. hypodermic

4. mesoderm

5. monocle

6. neural

7. neurotic

8. optical

9. orthopedics

10. osteoid

11. pathological

12. pedagogy

13. psychometrics

14. psychopath

15. tripod

SUPPLEMENTARY EXERCISE

Match that part of the body which would be suffering, with the proper medical term for the ailment. For your reference the Greek roots are also provided.

1. bronchitis (bronch) _____   a. belly, stomach

2. cardia disorder (kardia) _____   b. heart

3. dermatitis (derm) _____   c. kidney

4. a gastric ulcer (gast) _____   d. liver

5. hepatotoxic condition (hepa) _____   e. lungs

6. nephritis (nephr) _____   f. nerves

7. neurosis (neuro) _____   g. ribs

8. acute phlebitis (phleps) _____   h. skin

9. pleurisy (pleur) _____   i. throat

10. pneumonia (pneuma) _____   j. vein

LESSON 30

THE SCIENCES
FROM A TO Z

GREEK ROOTS FOUND
IN SCIENTIFIC TERMINOLOGY

Why could we not refer to members of the Audubon Society as "bird-watchers" instead of ornithologists? Or why could we not study the "lore of ancient civilizations" instead of archaeology? Would not the simplification of scientific terminology into more modern English make our studies of the sciences just a little easier? And then why must most of the words be of Greek derivation and almost unpronounceable?

There seem to be two logical responses to these and similar queries. First and foremost is the fact that a science should be international in scope. As opposed to the almost universally acceptable Greek term, *oxygen,* the German word *sauerstoff* (sour-stuff) is clearly provincial. Since ancient Greece had such a tremendous effect on the cultural and linguistic growth of the western world (both the original *schole* and the *akademia* were in Athens), and since ancient Greek has remained fairly constant, it has lent itself favorably to this aspect of universality. Secondly, as many of the sciences had their earliest development in ancient Greece, it seemed quite appropriate for such eminent scholars as Bacon, Copernicus, Newton, and others to retain some of the original "terminology" as they helped initiate the tremendous progress of the physical sciences in the sixteenth and seventeenth centuries. Moreover, although the typical "higher school" of the late middle ages was divided into the trivium, teaching grammar, rhetoric, and dialectic (philosophy) and the quadrivium, teaching the *scientiae* of *arithmetica, geometrica, astronomica* and *musica* (actually acoustic physics), the scientists frequently began to find themselves at odds with their clerical colleagues. Since the language of the church and the clerics was Latin, the scientists turned to the language of the earliest scientists, the Greeks, for their new and yet universally acceptable terminology. In "Bishop Blougram's Apology," Robert Browning expresses well this conflict:

165

> blot out cosmology,
> Geology, ethnology, what not,
> (Greek endings, each the little
> passing-bell
> That signifies some faith's about
> to die)

(lines 679-682)

Now let us look at some of the sciences which owe their names, if not their origins, to the Greeks. This is not intended to be a classification key of the sciences but rather a listing of roots which lend themselves to the unlocking of the meaning of other collegiate words.

Roots

Greek Roots	Meaning	Examples
anthrop	man	anthropology, philanthropic
arch	ancient, chief	archaeology, archaic
aster, astr	star	astronomer, astronomical
bio	life	biochemist, autobiography
cosm	order, universe	cosmology, cosmonaut
geo	earth	geology, geophysics
morph	form	morphology, metamorphosis
phil	love, like	philosopher, philharmonic
physic	nature	physics, physiology
the, theo	god	theology, theism
zo	animal	zoologist, protozoa

EXERCISE A

A MATTER OF CHOICE

From the "Examples" supply the missing word for each of the following sentences. The italicized words should provide you with a clue.

Example:

The science which deals with the *study* of the lore of *ancient civilizations* is (archaeology.)

1. The science which deals with the entire *study* of *man* is _____

   _____.

2. A *person* who *studies* the *stars* for the purpose of advising others as to their

   destinies or daily happenings has been called an _____.

3. The scientist whose task is to examine *chemical* compounds and their

   processes occurring in *living* organisms is known as a _____

   _____.

4. The branch of astronomy which deals specifically with the origin, order, and

   structure of the entire *universe* is _____.

5. A basic *course* which deals with the description of the physical features of

   the *earth* may be catalogued: Introduction to _____.

6. The study of the *formation* of a word, both as to its derivational and in-

   flectional processes, can be called its _____.

7. T. S. Eliot, because of his *fondness* for and his critical *study* of literature,

   was more noted as a _____ than as a poet.

8. Physics is a *natural* science dealing with matter, energy and their various

   interactionary aspects, while _____ deals pri-

   marily with the *study* of processes, activities and phenomena of *living*

   matter.

9. Seminarians and rabbinical students often choose to major in

   _____ so that their faith in *God* can be sup-

   ported by reason.

10. The specialist who is concerned with the *study* of *animal* life is a

    _____.

EXERCISE B

THE FINALE!

From your knowledge of the above roots, and previous affixes and roots, give a meaning for each of the italicized words. Check the dictionary after doing all ten.

1. . . . considered a *philanthropist*—

2. . . . an *archaic* and trite expression—

3. . . . the *astronomical* figure of the budget—

4. . . . a truly *autobiographical* account—

5. . . . the Russian *cosmonaut* met an instantaneous death—

6. . . . the *geophysical* condition discovered after the volcano—

7. . . . the *metamorphic* coal deposits—

8. . . . a doctor skilled in *physiotherapy*—

9. . . . the king's *theocratic* right to rule—

10. . . . evidenced *protozoic* characteristics—

ADDENDA

LISTS OF ROOTS AND AFFIXES

The knowledge of certain Latin and Greek roots and affixes provides you with a key which can unlock the meanings of many new words. One advantage of "Lists of Roots and Affixes" is that they make it easier for you to develop a richer and broader vocabulary. By studying various prefixes you may arrive at the meanings of many words. You are not learning words in isolation but rather groups of related words. Roots, especially those which were originally verbs, may have two or more forms. It was common in Latin for changes to occur in the formation of the verb's principal parts. Thus we have "fer," and "lat," both from the Latin verb *ferre*. Note the many words we can find based on these two forms:

confer	collate
defer	correlate
differ	elate
fertile	dilate
infer	legislate
interfere	oblate
offer	ventilation
prefer	prelate
refer	relate
transfer	translate

The general criterion for selection of a root or affix in this textbook was that it was found in at least ten different words.

Again, a word of caution regarding the use of etymology. Many words have been in the English language for many centuries and their modern meanings may bear little, if any, resemblance to the true meaning of the root.

For example, look at the word *precipitation*. Etymologically it developed:

(a) pre—before
(b) cipit—caput (L. meaning head)
(c) tion—the act of

The word usually refers to condensation (rain or snow) in the atmosphere. This is a far cry from "the head moving before the body."

The following five lists present the Latin and Greek elements used in this text. They are arranged in the order of their appearance in the textbook.

ADDENDUM 1

COMMON LATIN PREFIXES

In the following table of "The Common Latin Prefixes,"the most common prefixes are listed, their most general meanings given and examples of their use are provided. See if you can ascertain how each prefix has affected the meanings of the various roots. In some instances, those followed by an asterisk, the final consonant of the prefix may be changed to the initial consonant of the root or dropped completely.

Since the Latin numeral prefixes are treated in Lesson 13, they do not appear on this list.

Latin	Meaning	Examples
ab	from, off, away	abnegation
abs	from	abstract
a		aversely
ad*	to, towards	admonish
ac, af		accurately, affinity
ag, ap		aggregate, apprehensive
ambi	around, both	ambiguous, ambidextrous
ante	before, previous	antecedent, antediluvian
bene	good, well	benediction
beni		benignant
circum	around, about	circumlocution
circu		circulate
co*	with, together	cohort
con, com		congregate, complement
col, cor		collaborate, corruption
contra	against, opposite	contradict
contro		controversy
counter		counterattack
de	down, from, off, away	delineate, deductive
di	away, off, opposite	diverse
dif		diffident
dis		dissipate
e	out of, off,	egress
ex	away from	express
ef		effuse

171

Latin	Meaning	Examples
ex extra extro	former, beyond, outside of, exceptional	ex-husband, ex-officio extracurricular extrovert
in* im, il ir	not, opposing	invalid immature, illicit irrelevant
in il, im	in, into	induct illumination, immigrate
inter	among, between	intercept, interpret, intercollegiate
intra intro	inwardly, within	intravenous, intramural introvert
mal male	bad, evil, ill	malfunction malevolent
mis	wrong, ill	mislead, misspell, misfit
multi	many, much	multiplicity, multifarious
non	not	nonessential, noncombatant
ob* oc of, op	against, toward	obdurate occlude offensive, oppression
pen per	almost throughout, thoroughly	peninsula, penultimate persevere, permutation
post pre	after, behind before	postmortem, postscript predilection, previous
pro pur	forward, favoring, for	prodigious purchase
re retro se	back, again backward apart, away, aside	return, review retroactive, retrogress secede, secrete
sub, sus suc, suf sum, sup sur	under, beneath, slightly	submit, susceptible succumb, suffix summon, supplement surreptitious
super, sur	over, above, exceeding, extra	superimpose, surrealist
trans ultra un	across, beyond beyond, excessive not	transit, transgressor ultramodern, ultraviolet unprecedented, uninvited

ADDENDUM 2

COMMON SUFFIXES

Following are the lists of the most common suffixes with some of their general meanings and a few examples of each. You are not expected to memorize them, rather it is hoped that you will find occasions to refer to them in order to obtain a better understanding of difficult words and in order to be able to express yourself more precisely. The lists are separated into their parts of speech categories.

I. NOUN-FORMING SUFFIXES

Suffix	Meaning	Examples
age	act of, place, rank, state	breakage, hermitage
ance, ence	act, amount, condition, state	compliance, convalescence
ard, art	excessive	drunkard, braggart
ate	office, function rank	consulate, delegate
ation, ition, tion, ion	action, result, state	aggregation, addition, projection, coercion
cy, ancy, ency, ity, ty, y	condition, quality, state	potency, arrogancy, emergency, civility, deity, sympathy
dom	condition, state	kingdom, serfdom
ee	one performing an action / one receiving an action	payee, escapee
er, eer, or, ar	actor, maker, one who	kibitzer, racketeer, aviator, vicar
ese	of, relating to	Chinese, journalese
ess	female	governess, hostess
et, ette	small, feminine	cadet, dinette, coquette
ice	act, quality, state	benefice, malice
ism	act, doctrine, movement	Communism, narcissism
ling	quality of, young	hireling, duckling
ment	action, means, office, state	abridgement, ornament, excitement
ness	state of, quality of	goodness, appropriateness
ship	state of office, art, skill	apprenticeship, judgeship, statemenship

Suffix	Meaning	Examples
tude	act, condition, state of	latitude, multitude
ure	action, result, instrument	composure, exposure, nomenclature

II. ADJECTIVE-FORMING SUFFIXES

Suffix	Meaning	Examples
able, ible	capable of, given to	perishable, incorrigible
ate	having, showing	effeminate, temperate
en	made of, like, showing	earthen, deaden, enliven
escent	beginning, becoming	adolescent, effervescent
ful	full of	fruitful, hopeful
ish	like, suggesting	fetish, fiendish
less	lacking, without	dauntless, sinless
ous, ose	characteristic of, given to, quality of	efficacious, verbose
y, ey	characteristic of, showing, like	ebony, slimey

III. NOUN-ADJECTIVE-FORMING SUFFIXES

Suffix	Meaning	Examples
al	act of, characteristic of, pertaining to	radical, adjectival
an, ean, ian	belonging to, showing, pertaining to	American, Freudian, octogenarian
ant, ent	one who, showing	celebrant, diffident
ary, ery, ory	belonging to, showing, characteristic of	coronary, snobbery, accessory
fic	causing, like, relating to	prolific, pacific
ic, ac	causing, like, relating to	maniac, platonic
ine	characteristic of, made of, marked by	canine, pristine
ist	actor, believer, one who specializes	chauvinist, materialist,
ite	formed, marked by, native of, showing	partite, Brooklynite
ive	belonging to, tends toward	progressive, furtive

IV. VERB-FORMING SUFFIXES

Suffix	Meaning	Examples
ate	act on, cause, form, make	collate, segregate
en	become, cause	liken, lengthen
fy	cause, make	mortify, rectify
ize	cause, make	regularize, tantalize

V. ADVERB-FORMING SUFFIXES

Suffix	Meaning	Examples
ly	like, way, manner of	helplessly, aesthetically
wise	direction, way, manner	clockwise, moneywise

ADDENDUM 3

LATIN ROOTS

The following is a listing of the Latin Roots with their common meanings used in this textbook. Usually two examples of each root are provided. Where common alternative forms of the roots are available, a derivation of each is included so that you can more readily judge its development. For the most part elementary words have been avoided. The number in parentheses after a root indicates in which lesson the root was treated.

Root	Origin	Meaning	Examples
ag, act (23)	agere	do, drive	agility, agitation, interaction
alter, altr (19)	alter	other, change	altercation, altruism
anim (17)	animus	mind, soul, spirit	inanimate, unanimous
aud (16)	audire	to hear	audile, audition
cad, cis, cid (24)	cadere	to fall	cadence, decadent, casualty, coincidence
cap, capt, cept, cip (22)	capere	to take, to seize	capability, captions susceptible, emancipation
capit, cipit (17)	caput	head, main	capitulate, precipitation
card, cord (17)	cor (cordis)	heart	cardiogram, cordially
carn (17)	caro (carnis)	flesh	carnivorous, incarnate
cede, ceed, cess (20)	cedere	to go, to yield	antecedent, intercession, proceeding, recede
cert (24)	certare	to decide, to make certain	certification, concerted
cide, cis (22)	caedere, (cecide)	to cut, to kill	homicide, conciseness, excise
claus, clus, clud (19)	claudere	to close	claustrophobia, inclusive, occlude
cred (18)	credere	to believe, to trust	credence, incredulous
cres, cre, cret (24)	crescere	to grow	crescendo, increment, secretion
curr, curs (21)	currere	to run	concurrent, cursory, extracurricular
dent (17)	dens (dentis)	tooth	dentrifice, indenture
dic, dict (16)	dicere (dictum)	to speak	abdication, dictatorial, verdict

176

Root	Origin	Meaning	Examples
doc, doct (24)	docere	to teach, to prove	docile, documentary, indoctrinate
duc, duct (20)	ducere (ductum)	to lead	conducive, abduction, deduction
ego (19)	ego	I, self	egocentric, egotist
equ (21)	aequus	equal, same	equate, equilibrium
fac, fact fect, fic, (16)	facere (factum)	to do, to make	facsimile, faction, affectation, fiction
fer, lat (21)	ferre (latum)	to carry, to bear	interfere, vociferous, sublation
fid (18)	fides	faith	confidant, infidelity
flu, fluct, flux (19)	fluere	to flow	affluent, fluctuate, influx
frag, fract (21)	frangere (fractum)	to break	fragile, refractory
grad, gred gress (20)	gradi	to step	gradually, ingredient, aggression
hab, hib (23)	habere	to have, to hold	habitual, rehabilitate, inhibit
her, hes (23)	haerere	to cling, to stick	adhere, inherent, cohesion
jac, ject (19)	jacere	to throw	ejaculate, reject, subject
jug, junct (18)	jungere	to join	conjugal, adjunct, juncture
leg, lect, lig (23)	legere	to choose	elegance, electoral, eligible
leg (22)	lex (legis)	law	legislature, illegitimate
locu, loqu (16)	loqui	to speak	elocution, loquacious, soliloquy
man, manu (17)	manus	hand	emancipation, manual, manuscript
mis, mit (20)	mittere	to send	missionary, submissive, permit
mon, monit (23)	monere	to warn	summon, admonition
mot, mov, mob (24)	movere (motum)	to move	promote, removal, mobilize
mor, mort (22)	mors (mortis)	death	moribund, immortality, mortified
ocul (17)	oculus	eye	oculist, binocular
ora (18)	orare	to play	oracle, oration
ped (17)	pes (pedis)	foot	impediment, pedestrian
pel, puls (23)	pellere	to drive, to push	appellate, impel, compulsion
pend, pens, pond (22)	pendere (pondus)	to hang, to weigh	appendix, pendulum, pensive, ponder
pet, pit (23)	petere	to seek	competitor, petition, propitious

Root	Origin	Meaning	Examples
pon, pos (21)	ponere	to put, to place	component, proponent, opposite
port (20)	portare	to carry	portable, transport
quir, ques, quis (23)	quaerere	to search out	inquire, questionable, prerequisite
rupt (19)	rumpere	to break	corruption, disruptive
seg, sect (21)	secare (secutum)	to cut	segment, dissect
scrib, script (16)	scribere	to write	proscribe, transcribe, scripture
sed, sid (16)	sedere	to sit	sedentary, sediment, insidious
sequ, secut sue (23)	sequi	to follow	consequence, obsequious, persecute, ensue
spec, spect, spic (16)	spectare	to watch, to look at	speculate, retrospect, perspicuous
stru, struct (24)	struere	to build	misconstrue, instruction, obstruct
sta, stat, (sist) (23)	stare	to stand	instability, obstacle, statute, persistence
tang, ting, (21) tact	tangere	to touch	tangible, contingent, tactile
temp, (24) tempor	tempus, temporis	time	contemporary, extemporaneous
ten, tin, tain (18)	tenere	to hold	lieutenant, tenacious, pertinent, retainer
tend, tens, tent (24)	tendere	to stretch	tendency, tension, pretentious
tol (21)	tollere	to endure	tolerate, extol
tors, tort (22)	torquere	to twist	contorsion, distort
tract (22)	trahere	to draw, to drag	distract, intractible
us, ut (24)	uti (usum)	to use	abusive, usury, utensil
vad, vas (20)	vadare	to wander	pervade, evasive
ven, vent (20)	venire	to come	intervene, revenue, convention
vers, vert (19)	vertere	to turn	advertisement, versatile, introvert
vid, vis, vi (24)	videre (visum)	to see	evident, revise, enviable
vinc, vinct (23)	vincere	to conquer	invincible, conviction
viv, vit (18)	vivere	to live	vivacious, vitality
voc, vok (16)	vocare (vocatum)	to call	convocation, irrevocable, invoke

ADDENDUM 4

COMMON GREEK PREFIXES

Following is a list of some of the more common Greek prefixes. You are not expected to memorize them; rather, you should endeavor to become familiar with them and be able to refer to this list when the occasion arises.

Prefix	Meanings	Examples
a, an	lacking, without	agnostic, anesthesia
ana	against, back	analytic, anachronism
anti, ant	against, opposite	antagonist, anti-climactic
apo	away from, separate	apostate, apology
cata	down, thoroughly	catalog, cataract
dia	across, through	diameter, diagnostic
en, em	in, among	encyclical, empirical
epi	after, over	epilogue, episode
eu	good, well	eugenics, eulogize
homo	same	homogeneous, homograph
hyper	excessive	hyperactive, hyperbole
hypo	beneath, under	hypodermic, hypocrisy
mega	large	megapolis, megaphone
meta	change	metaphor, metabolism
micro	small	microscope, microbiology
neo	new	neophyte, neolithic
ortho	straight, correct	orthography, orthodox
pan	all	panacea, pantheist
para, par	beside, beyond	paradox, parody
peri	around	perimeter, periscope
poly	many	polygon, polyclinic
syn, sym	together, with	synonym, symbolic
tele	far, distance	telegraph, telephone

ADDENDUM 5

GREEK ROOTS

Root	Origin	Meaning	Example
agog agogue (28)	agein	to lead	demagogue, synagogue
anthrop (30)	anthropos	man	anthropology, philanthropist
arch (30)	archaios	ancient, chief	archaic, monarch
aster, astr (30)	aster	star	astrology, astronomical
auto (28)	autos	self	automatic, autonomy
bio (30)	bios	life	biochemist, biopsy
chiro (29)	chir	hand	chiropractor, chiropodist
chron (27)	chronos	time	anachronism, chronicle
cosm (30)	cosmos	order, universe	cosmic, cosmonaut
crac, crat (28)	cratia	rule, power	aristocracy, democrat
dem (28)	demos	people	demagogue, endemic
derm (29)	derma	skin	dermatologist, epidermis
don (29)	don	tooth	orthodontist
dox (28)	doxa (dokein)	belief	orthodox, paradox
gen (28)	genos	kind, race	eugenics, genesis
geo (30)	ge	earth	geometry, geology
gon (27)	gonia	side, angle	diagonal, trigonometry
gram, graph (27)	graphein	to write	epigram, graphic
iatr (29)	iatrikos	cure (to heal)	geriatrics, psychiatrist
log (27)	logos	study, speech	catalog, monologue
meter, metr (27)	metron	measure	centimeter, symmetry
morph (30)	morphe	form	amorphous, metamorphosis
neur (29)	neuron	nerve, tendon	neuralgia, neurotic
nom (27)	nomos	law, rule	autonomy, monograph
onym (27)	onyma	name	anonymous, pseudonym
optic, opt (29)	optikos	eye	optical, synopsis
osteo (29)	osteon	bone	osteopath, osteotomy
path (29)	pathos	feeling, suffering	apathy, pathology
ped (29)	pais (paid)	child	pediatrician, orthopedic
phil (30)	philos	love, like	philharmonic, philosophy
phon, phono (27)	phonos	sound	dictaphone, symphony

Root	Origin	Meaning	Example
physi (30)	phisis	nature	physician, physiology
pod, pus (29)	podos	foot	podiatrist, octopus
psych (29)	psyche	mind	psychoanalysis, psychiatry
pyr, pyro (28)	pyr	fire	pyromania, pyrotechnics
scope (27)	skopein	to see, to watch	microscopic, telescope
tax, tac (28)	tassein	to arrange	syntax, tactics
the (30)	theos	God	atheism, theology
zo (30)	zoon	animal	protozoa, zodiac

EXERCISE A

LESSON 1–30

Lesson 1, Exercise A

Definitions may vary:

a. place for studying
b. humbug, meaningless
c. terse, short
d. very small
e. walk aimlessly
f. tourist attraction
g. wild disorder
h. dark, gloomy
i. given to luxury
j. impractical

1. lilliputian
2. pandemonium
3. meandering
4. mecca
5. utopian
6. laconic
7. anthenaeum
8. bunkum
9. sybarite
10. stygian

Lesson 2, Exercise A

Definitions may vary:

a. dew
b. drunken revelry
c. pertaining to sexual desires
d. warlike
e. changeableness
f. drug for lessening pain
g. a formidable rival
h. monster
i. a gentle breeze

1. erotic
2. ogre
3. jovial
4. nemesis
5. aurora's tears
6. martial
7. bacchanalian
8. morphine
9. mercurial
10. zephyr

Lesson 3, Exercise A

1. junta
2. cherubs
3. guerrilla
4. apartheid
5. kosher
6. hinterland
7. boudoir
8. dilettante
9. blitzkreig
10. fiasco

Lesson 4, Exercise A

1. ex officio
2. coup d'état
3. cul-de-sac
4. nom de plume
5. deus ex machina
6. hoi polloi
7. sine qua non
8. faux pas
9. vis à vis
10. sub rosa

Lesson 5, Exercise A

1. without an equal
2. in the middle of the situation
3. reference guide books
4. clear cut, pointed
5. rogue, vagabond
6. purification
7. outcome
8. contrived solution
9. the exact word
10. words, blended to make one word

Lesson 6, Exercise A

1. avant-garde
2. brainwash
3. coup de grâce

4. digital computer
5. devil-may-care
6. east-southeast
7. featherbedding
8. laissez-faire
9. living wage
10. mass media
11. no-man's-land
12. par excellence
13. sixty-fourth
14. tax-exempt
15. tripod

Lesson 7, Exercise A

1. C
2. A
3. C
4. B
5. B
6. C
7. A
8. B
9. C
10. A

Lesson 8, Exercise A

Part I

1. armor
2. cigarette
3. demon
4. dialogue
5. louver
6. nosy
7. offense
8. plow
9. theater
10. visor

Part II

1   3   4   5   7   10

Lesson 9, Exercise A

1. analyses
2. beliefs
3. soliloquies
4. aides-de-camp
5. worst
6. least
7. politicking
8. referred, conference
9. more bizarre
10. loosened

Lesson 10, Exercise A

Answers will vary.

1. (a) A pitched ball that the catcher can reasonably be expected to catch, but misses.
   (b) A ball thrown by a backfield man, usually the quarterback, to an end or to another backfield man.
   (c) A linesman on the football team whose position is between the guard and the end, and whose responsibility is to tackle or block for the ball carrier.
   (d) The gear or materials used in fishing.
2. England (British)
3. wildly active or lively
4. Roman Catholics
5. NCD, NWD, Colloquial; ACD, SCD-Illiterate or Dialect; RHDC-Non-Standard
6. Chemist
7. In British speaking country
8. Student on a scholarship at Oxford from the British Commonwealth or the United States
9. In math., a sign ($\sqrt{}$) placed before an expression to denote that the square root is to be extracted. In hist., a person of a political group with views, practices, and policies of extreme change.
10. no

Lesson 11, Exercise A

1. postbellum
2. inductive
3. interior
4. emigrate
5. superior
6. extrovert
7. benignant
8. defensive
9. progress
10. prefix

Lesson 12, Exercise A

1. annulment
2. component
3. diffident

4. effeminacy
5. incorrigible
6. illogical
7. immerse
8. occultism
9. succumb
10. subdominant

Lesson 13, Exercise A

1. 8
2. 3, including the original
3. 4
4. alone, by itself
5. 5 year
6. ninth
7. 9 months
8. tenth
9. oneness
10. ten (70 days)

Lesson 14, Exercise A

1. frustration
2. perseverance
3. conciseness
4. draftee
5. refusal
6. incorruptibility
7. despondency
8. timidness, timidity
9. secession
10. legislature

Lesson 15, Exercise A

1. equipping
2. bountiful
3. noticeably
4. recurrently
5. colonial
6. depletion
7. incitement
8. conjecturability
9. concreteness
10. manageable
11. decayed
12. penniless
13. immensely
14. relievable
15. acquitance
16. auspicious
17. aspirator
18. decreasingly
19. submergence
20. foreclosure

187

Lesson 16, Exercise A

1. auditor
2. invoked
3. soliloquy
4. transcript
5. abdication
6. avocation
7. facsimile
8. interdict
9. proscribes
10. sedentary
11. loquacious
12. insidious
13. pacification
14. audile
15. speculate

Lesson 17, Exercise A

Answers will vary.

1. heart shaped
2. measuring instrument
3. handcuffs
4. type of eyeglass
5. strong dislike
6. great destruction of life
7. use of both eyes
8. steep place
9. halt, delay
10. agreement

Lesson 18, Exercise A

1. F
2. F
3. F
4. T
5. T
6. T
7. T
8. F
9. F
10. F

Lesson 19, Exercise A

1. altruist
2. precluded
3. corruption
4. fluent
5. rejected
6. alternative
7. subject
8. secluded
9. I, center
10. reverse

Lesson 20, Exercise A

1. D
2. H
3. J
4. E
5. I

6. G
7. B
8. A
9. F
10. C

Lesson 21, Exercise A

1. equilibrium
2. transfer
3. proponent
4. composite
5. fragile

6. contingency
7. segment
8. tolerate
9. fragmented
10. current

Lesson 22, Exercise A

Killing of:

1. brother
2. germs
3. infant
4. insect
5. mother

6. father
7. pests
8. king
9. self
10. viruses

Lesson 23, Exercise A

1. rehabilitation
2. petulant
3. prerequisites
4. inherent
5. desist

6. appellant
7. reactionary
8. ensuing
9. ineligible
10. admonition

Lesson 24, Exercise A

Answers will vary.

1. rushing, falling
2. agreement in planning
3. increase or growth
4. instructed thoroughly
5. wire construction in motion
6. at the same time
7. emphasis, force
8. means or agent
9. take over by force
10. being prepared beforehand

Lesson 25, Exercise A

1. F
2. T
3. F
4. F
5. T
6. T
7. T
8. F
9. T
10. F
11. T
12. T
13. F

14. F
15. T
16. T
17. T
18. F
19. T
20. F
21. T
22. T
23. F
24. F
25. T

Lesson 26, Exercise A

1. trilogy
2. monologue
3. ennead
4. dichotomy
5. pentameter

6. tetraoxide
7. heptarchy
8. Ten Command-
   ments.
9. hexapod
10. hemisphere

Lesson 27, Exercise A

1. chronological
2. telegraph
3. monologue
4. trigonometry
5. perimeter

6. pentagon
7. astronomer
8. phonics
9. microscope
10. anonymous

Lesson 28, Exercise A

Part I

1. coin-operated cafeteria
2. no answer
3. an expression of praise to God
4. policeman
5. science that deals with improvement of hereditary qualities of a race or breed
6. no answer
7. fire
8. one who prepares, stuffs, and mounts animal skins
9. involving limited military action
10. no answer

Part II

11. C
12. D
13. E
14. A
15. F

Lesson 29, Exercise A

1. dermatologist
2. neurologist
3. orthodontist
4. chiropractor
5. optometrist (ophthalmologist)
6. psychologist
7. pathologist
8. pediatrician
9. osteopath
10. podiatrist

Lesson 30, Exercise A

1. anthropology
2. astronomer
3. biochemist
4. cosmology
5. geology
6. morphology
7. philosopher
8. physics
9. theology
10. zoologist

REFERENCES

Armstrong, Spencer. *How Words Get Into the Dictionary.* New York: Funk and Wagnalls Co., 1949.

Asimov, Isaac. *Words of Science and the History Behind Them.* Boston: Houghton Mifflin Co., 1959.

Bloomfield, Leonard. *Language.* New York: Holt, 1961.

Fowler, H. W. *A Dictonary of Modern American Usage.* New York: Oxford University Press, 1965.

Gray, Jack C. *Words, Words, and Words About Dictionaries.* San Francisco: Chadler, 1963.

Groom, Bernard. *A Short History of English Words.* London: Macmillan Co., 1965.

Higbet, Gilbert. *Changing Words.* New York: Oxford University Press, 1957.

Hogben, Lancelot. *The Loom of Languages.* New York: Norton Co., 1944.

Hughes, John P. *The Science of Language.* New York: Random House, 1964.

Hunt, Cecil. *Word Origins: The Romance of Language.* New York: Philosophical Library Inc., 1962.

Laird, Charlton. *The Miracle of Language.* New York: Fawcett World Library, 1963.

Lambert, Eloise. *Our Language: The Story of the Words We Use.* New York: Lathrop, Lee and Shepard Co., 1955.

Marchwardt, Albert H. *Introduction to the English Language.* New York: Oxford University Press, 1966.

Newmark, Maxim. *Dictionary of Foreign Words.* New Jersey: Littlefield, Adams and Co., 1965.

Pei, Mario. *The Families of Words.* New York: Harper and Row, 1962.

Pollack, Thomas and William Baker. *The University Spelling Book.* New York: Prentice-Hall Inc., 1965.

Shipley, Joseph T. *Dictionary of Word Origins.* New Jersey: Littlefield, Adams and Co., 1965.

Smith, Robert W. L. *Dictionary of English Word-Roots.* New Jersey: Littlefield, Adams and Co., 1967.

Wedeck, Harry E. *Short Dictionary of Classical Word Origins.* New York: Philosophical Library Inc., 1957.

MAY